GCSE

Questions and Answers

ENGLISH
KEY STAGE 4

Ian Barr Chief Examiner
Chris Walton English Teacher

SERIES EDITOR: BOB McDUELL

Letts
EDUCATIONAL

First published 1995
Reprinted 1995 (twice)

Letts Educational
Aldine House
Aldine Place
London W12 8AW

Text: © Ian Barr and Chris Walton 1995

Design and illustrations: © BPP (Letts Educational) Ltd 1995

British Library Cataloguing in Publication Data

A CIP record for this book is available from the British Library.

ISBN 1 85758 317 5

Acknowledgements

Questions on p19, p23, p69: Reproduced by kind permission of the University of Cambridge Local Examinations Syndicate. Questions on p56 and p65: Reproduced by kind permission of the Midland Examining Group. The University of Cambridge Local Examinations Syndicate and the Midland Examining Group bear no responsibility for the example answers to questions taken from their past questions papers which are contained in this publication. Question on p54: Reproduced by kind permission of the Southern Examining Group. Any answers are the sole responsibility of the author and have not been provided or approved by the Southern Examining Group. Question on p56: Reproduced by kind permission of the Northern Examinations and Assessment Board. The author is responsible for any solutions or commentaries given, and these may not necessarily constitute the only possible solutions. Question on p58: Reproduced by kind permission of the Welsh Joint Education Committee. Question on p59: Reproduced by kind permission of the Scottish Examining Board. Any solutions to questions do not emanate from the Scottish Examining Board. Question on p61: Reproduced by kind permission of the University of London Examinations and Assessment Council. The University of London Examinations and Assessment Council accepts no responsibility what so ever for the accuracy or method of working in the answers given. Extract on p16 reproduced from an article by John Patten. Extract on p20 reproduced by arrangement with Watts Books, a division of the Watts Publishing Group, London from Life Guides: *The Environment and Health* by Brian Ward. Extract on pp24–5 reproduced from *Pole to Pole* by Michael Palin with the permission of BBC Enterprises Limited. Extract on p31–2 reproduced from *This Time Next Week* by Leslie Thomas, published by Pan Books Limited. *A Moment of Respect* on p32 reproduced by kind permission of Edwin Brock. "Mysterious Fireball Blasts Siberia" and "Monster in Lake Nyos" reproduced from *Giant Disasters*, published by Reader's Digest Association Inc. Article on pp46–7 © Times Newspapers Ltd. 1994. Extract on p52 reproduced from *Chelsea Child* by Rose Gamble with the permission of BBC Enterprises Limited. Extract on pp53–4 reproduced from *Homecoming* by William McIlvanney, published by Hodder & Stoughton. Article on p55 reproduced by kind permission of The Guardian. Extract on pp57–8 adapted from *Some Day My Prince Will Come* by Deborah Moggach. Extract on pp60–1 reproduced from *Flag on the Island* by V S Naipaul, published by André Deutsch. Extract on pp66–7 reproduced from *Boomerang* by Farukh Dondy, published by Victor Gollancz. Article on p68 reproduced from The Independent. Articles on p70 and p73 reproduced from the Evening Standard Magazine. Article on p71 reproduced from The Sunday Times. Article on p72 reproduced by permission of the publisher, The BLA Group Ltd, from *Foresight*, the magazine for Sun Alliance customers. Photograph on p42 reproduced by kind permission of the Geoscience Feature Picture Library. Photograph on p46 reproduced by kind permission of Hulton Deutsch. Photograph on p59 reproduced by kind permission of Dr William B Currie & Associates.

Page make-up by Jordan Publishing Design

Printed in Great Britain by Ashford Colour Press

Letts Educational is the trading name of BPP (Letts Educational) Ltd

Contents

HOW TO USE THIS BOOK

The aim of this book is to provide you, the student, with the help you need to reach the highest level of achievement possible in one of your most important examinations – the General Certificate of Secondary Education (GCSE) or, in Scotland, at General and Credit levels. The book is designed to help all students, up to and including A* grade at GCSE.

The *Questions and Answers* series is based on the belief that experienced Examiners can provide, through examination questions, sample answers and advice, the help a student needs to secure success.

Students often find it useful to plan their revision according to some predetermined pattern, during which weaknesses can be identified and eliminated so that confidence can grow, and so the primary consideration has been to present the main principles on which study can be based.

The *Questions and Answers* series is designed to provide:

- Easy-to-use **Revision summaries** which identify important information which the student must understand if progress is to be made answering examination questions. Spend some time on this section first and refer back to it whenever you find it necessary. There should not be anything in this section which is brand new; you will find that you have covered all the things referred to in class, but it will be useful to remind yourself of all the things covered in this section.

- Advice on the **different types of task** (or question) and how to answer them well to obtain the highest marks. We have included in the book a range of different types of task using **different types of stimulus material**. In one sense the technique you should use is always the same – read the stimulus material carefully, make notes, think and then complete the task taking care to revise your first attempt. However, associated with each task, or set of tasks, are specific notes which should help you both in approaching what you have to do and in reviewing what you have done.

- Information about other skills which will be tested on examination papers apart from the recall of knowledge. These are sometimes called **Assessment Objectives**. Modern GCSE examinations put great emphasis on the testing of objectives other than knowledge and understanding. Assessment objectives include communication, problem solving, evaluation and interpretation.

- The book contains many examples of **examination questions**. A student can improve by studying a sufficiently wide range of questions providing they are shown the way to improve their answers to these questions. Some of the questions come from actual examination papers or specimen materials published by Examination Boards. Other questions have been written by Examiners and aim to mirror closely real examination questions set by Examination Boards. The questions meet the requirements of all British Examination Boards.

- There are **sample answers** to some of the questions. They are not perfect answers but they point the way forward for you and perhaps they challenge you to do better. We would suggest that you might consider having a go at some of the tasks before reading the sample answers and then comparing what you have written with the sample answer. Without doubt this will give you food for thought. Remember, though, that there are rarely right or wrong answers in English.

- **Advice from Examiners**. By using the experience of actual Examiners we are able to give advice which can enable the student to see how their answers can be improved and success be ensured.

ASSESSMENT OBJECTIVES IN ENGLISH

Assessment objectives are linked very closely with the **Attainment Targets** of the National Curriculum and it is easiest to look at them in detail by linking them with those Attainment Targets.

Objective 1

- You must be able to demonstrate that you can speak about personal experiences and be able to express your views and feelings.
- You must be able to discuss things in a group and show that you can express your own views and also listen to the views of others.
- You must be able to explain things clearly.
- You must be able to demonstrate that you can work with a group to make a presentation.
- You must be able to show that you understand that how you speak may well change according to your audience and your intentions.

Objective 2

- You must be able to show that you have read a wide range of books and that you can speak about them. Some of them will be works of literature but some of them will be non-fiction.
- You must also show that you have read material from the media, newspapers and magazines, and understand why things are written in a particular way.
- You must be able to extract information from different texts and use that information.

Objective 3

- You must show that you can write in different ways for different purposes and can plan your writing, by writing in paragraphs and using correct punctuation.
- You must be able to show that you can use a range of suitable vocabulary.
- You must show that you know how to revise, edit and improve your writing.

Objective 4

- You must be able to write clearly and spell correctly.
- You must show that you understand the importance of presentation.

The *Questions and Answers* series helps you to develop skills and your abilities to meet these assessment objectives by use of questions and by examining possible answers and commenting on them. You might refer to the assessment objectives to help you answer the basic question, "What am I required to do?"

EXAMINATION TECHNIQUE

Success in GCSE examinations comes from proper preparation and a positive attitude to the examination. This book is intended to help you overcome "examination nerves" which often come from a fear of not being properly prepared. Examination technique is extremely important and certainly affects your performance. Remember the basics:

- Read the questions carefully.

- Make sure that you watch the time carefully and complete the paper. It is no good answering one question well if you spend so long doing it that you do not answer another question at all.

- Make sure that you answer the right number of questions. Read the rubric on the front of the examination paper carefully and keep it in mind.

- Examination papers usually tell you how many marks are available for each answer. Take notice of this information as the number of marks gives a guide to the importance of the question and often to the amount which you ought to write.

- Remember to leave time to check through your work carefully.

Use this book for practice and to gain confidence! Good Luck!

English is not the same as maths and science. It is not as if you can revise all that you have learnt in the hope that the topics will appear in questions on the exam paper.

However, you can so easily throw marks away in English exams by being careless or slovenly. The idea of these revision summaries is to help you eliminate all those silly errors. The aim is to help you to become accurate. Use the summaries to remind you of some of the approaches you need to perform well in written tasks, and of some of the technical points in the composition of writing, but remember that you will only be accurate if you make an effort to get things right in your own work.

SPELLING

You are not allowed to take a dictionary or spell-check into the examinations, but you should use them when you are doing your coursework.

You cannot be expected to spell every word in the English language correctly. However, regular use of a dictionary during your course will help you to master spelling.

Half the battle with accurate spelling is to avoid **careless** errors. To put this point another way, it is important that **you should want to get spellings right!** Be aware of careless errors; check over your work; always be thinking about spellings. At the very least this may help you to cut down the number of errors you make.

There are some very basic spellings which cause confusion. Sometimes they are spellings of words which sound similar but in fact mean something very different. Here are some examples of simple words which are often misspelt:

there, they're, their,

wear, we're, were, where,

no, know, now,

it's, its,

how, who,

whose, who's.

You are going to create a very poor impression if you make these simple errors. Make sure you have learnt the differences. Here are examples to help you learn them:

There are important exams next week. The pupils taking the exams hope **they're** going to pass.

They have been told that they will get **their** results in the Summer.

Cricketers **wear** whites for the match.

The commentator said, "Let's hope **we're** in for a good match!"

Where is the match being played?

Everybody will **know** about the party. There will be **no** food left over.

Now the music can start.

It's nearly time for the holidays.

The school finished **its** term early. (Some hopes!)

How easy is it to play tennis? There are some people **who** will say that it is very easy.

It was difficult to decide **whose** service was better.

I am sure that she is the player **who's** going to win.

Write out one example for each of these simple words, in order to make sure that you can get them right.

To move towards the higher grades in English you need to be able to use an appropriate and extensive vocabulary. You also need to be able to write in the form of Standard English, which will affect your choice of vocabulary. This section is presented as some questions and answers to help you think about vocabulary.

What can I do to develop my vocabulary in a piece of writing?
Always be thinking of alternatives. Never just accept the first word that comes to mind. Never use words sloppily, which do not mean much (e.g. "get" or "nice").

What is meant by "appropriate" vocabulary?
This means choosing the right tone of word. For a report or a formal letter you should not use colloquialisms or slang ("well-good" or "wicked"). Indeed in this kind of writing you should try to be as precise as possible. In a more imaginative piece you might well choose to use colloquialisms or slang, for effect.

What else can I do to achieve an appropriate vocabulary?
Try to vary your use of words, and avoid repetition, especially in the same sentence or paragraph. Remember that by using adjectives (words which describe nouns) and adverbs (words which describe verbs, usually ending in -ly), you can add to the precision of your writing.

How can I extend my vocabulary?
By becoming more interested in the meanings of words, usually through wide reading. In the period approaching your exam, why not read the newspaper for interest? You may have a lot of work to do, but continue reading books, right up to the last minute before your exam. You will continue to take in vocabulary.

Now for a word or two about **clichés**. A cliché is an overworked phrase or word. It is the sort of thing which has been said or written hundreds of times before, and, as a result, when you use it it does not mean anything. Stories sometimes start with: "It was a bright summer day… " Can you see why this is a cliché? Or: "The clouds looked like cotton wool… ".

How can I avoid clichés in my writing?
This will depend on the kind of writing that you are doing. If it is an imaginative piece, try to picture precisely what you are describing. Always try to visualise your events or scenes. If it is an informative piece, try to be clear precisely what you are arguing or stating. On paper, in rough, or in your head, go over the points you are making before you write them down. This should give you a better chance of choosing the most appropriate words.

Should I try to learn new words?
Well, there is no point in forcing out words onto the page if they are just there for effect! That can appear silly. There is a lot to be said for using a thesaurus, however, especially when doing coursework. Above all, a thesaurus can make you enthusiastic for new words.

When you write you need to use paragraphs for TWO main reasons:

1 your ideas must be organised;

2 you will make it easier for the reader to follow what you are writing (how important is this in an exam?!)

What is a paragraph?
A paragraph is a section of writing. Writers stop after they have covered a point, or a series of related points, and at a suitable moment, start a new section. When we write in handwriting, which we always do in an exam, we **indent** the start of our new paragraphs. (You will find that this

happens in books although increasingly writers using word processors are not indenting in all documents.) **YOU MUST INDENT!!** However, there is an exception: there is no need to indent the **first paragraph** of a story or essay.

What do we mean by indent? Look at where I positioned the "w" in the first word of this sentence. What do you notice about it? It is slightly moved in from the margin. If you find it difficult to remember to do this, you could also leave a line between one paragraph and the next. You will find helpful examples of the layout of paragraphs in the extracts from the Stimulus material and Exam practice sections of this book. Have a good look at these and make sure you understand how paragraphs are set out.

What do you need to do to make sure that you are using paragraphs?

❶ Use your plan. You do not necessarily need to number each paragraph but it helps if you have been able to **jot down your points in a sequence** which can then form each paragraph. Keep looking back at your plan as this can provide you with a guide for your paragraphs.

❷ As you are writing, think about the **organisation of ideas, events, descriptions, arguments, key points etc.** OK, so it is difficult! A lot of pupils say that they forget to use paragraphs because they are lost in thought. They are too tied up with the ideas in their writing. So try to look up every now and again. **Step back from the page and ask yourself questions about the layout of your work.** I find it helpful to think of it like painting a picture. If your eye is too close to the canvas, you cannot see the whole picture. You need to look at the arrangement of objects in the work, as well as the detail.

How many paragraphs and how often?

There are no easy answers to this question. If you have too many paragraphs and they are then too short, it will suggest that your ideas are too shallow, too simple. On the other hand, overlong paragraphs will make you guilty of inadequate organisation. **You must strike a balance!** One area where you need regular paragraphing is when you are reporting speech in a story. For revision of this see the following revision summary which is on punctuation.

PUNCTUATION

When you write you need to use punctuation for THREE main reasons:

❶ you can show the relationships between one part of a sentence and another;

❷ you can help to stress emphasis or tone in what you are writing;

❸ you will be able to organise your work.

What punctuation do you need to be able to use?

FULL STOPS: to mark the ends of sentences. But do not break down your writing into sentences which are too short! That's too easy!

COMMAS: for a variety of reasons; to mark off one clause from the remainder of the sentence; to establish a pause; to give one word or a few words special emphasis.

CONFUSION BETWEEN FULL STOPS AND COMMAS: sometimes it is easy to confuse the use of commas and full stops. As a general rule any sentence should contain **only one MAIN verb**. If you realise that you are about to start a new "unit of sense", then use a full stop and start a new sentence. Never use a comma loosely when you are really starting a new sentence. However, try to combine or merge sentences to make them more complex – for this you will need the comma regularly.

COLONS AND SEMI-COLONS: Colons (:) are used to introduce lists or to introduce main points of discussion and argument. There are many examples of colons on this page. **Semi-colons (;)** are used to join together two sentences that are very close in their meanings or as a replacement for commas when separating points in a list.

QUESTION MARKS AND EXCLAMATION MARKS: Question marks (?) always end a sentence which asks a question. Note that a question mark contains its own full stop and does not require another one. **Exclamation marks (!)** should be used at the end of a sentence which expresses something very strongly or humorously. But use them sparingly. Too many of them can ruin the effect for the reader.

SPEECH MARKS: also known as **inverted commas** or **quotation marks**, they exist to punctuate **direct** or **reported speech** and also for **titles** and **quotations**. There are some basic guidelines: place the marks at the start and finish of all the speech, including all other marks of punctuation; following the words spoken, when you return to the narrative, continue the sentence – do not use capital letters; if you are reporting the speech of more than one speaker follow the rules of paragraphing, starting each new speaker on a new line and indenting the first words. Remember what was said about paragraphing on pp 5–6.

HYPHENS: for joining words or parts of words; **DASHES:** for separating words or phrases for a particular effect; **BRACKETS:** for marking off phrases or words which are additional to the main sentence (often asides, clarifications, alternatives etc.); **APOSTROPHES:** see the following section.

There are TWO types of apostrophe:

❶ the apostrophe of omission;

❷ the apostrophe of possession.

THE APOSTROPHE OF OMISSION: for use when you are writing a word or combination of words which have been **contracted** and you have left out a letter or more than one letter. This should not be difficult to understand. Simply replace the letter or letters that have been left out with an apostrophe (').

Here are some common contractions in everyday use: it's… he's… we'll… don't… can't.

In each of the above words, which letters have been omitted?

There is another type of omission. This is when you are reporting the way characters speak in a realistic way and you wish to represent accent or dialect.

E.g. 'e's really bin workin' 'ard to pass 'is exams!

THE APOSTROPHE OF POSSESSION (OR POSSESSIVE APOSTROPHE): for use when, in the grammar of your sentence, something belongs to another word, or is literally possessed by another word. This apostrophe is usually called the **apostrophe s**. There are differences between where you place the **apostrophe s** according to whether you have a singular noun "owner" or a plural noun "owner". There is a simple way of remembering the difference. Singular nouns have **'s** and plural nouns have **s'** at the end of the word. Study the difference in the examples below:

For **singular** nouns: The **pupil's** books.
The **girl's** pen.

For **plural** nouns: The **athletes'** times. (There is more than one athlete)
The **boys'** games. (There is more than one boy.)

For plural nouns which do not end in "s": The **women's** coats
The **gentlemen's** outfitter.

One word which always causes confusion: its – when you use the word **its** as a possessive pronoun, it does not require a possessive apostrophe. Neither do **his, her, their, our**… so do not be tempted to use one with **its**.

E.g The dog returns to **its** bone.
The tree sheds **its** leaves.

See above, in the section on the apostrophe of omission, for the use of the word **it's**.

SPEECH MARKS

1 When the speech comes first:

"There was a huge fire in our road last night," said the worried child.

What to look out for: all the words spoken are contained within the inverted commas; the punctuation (comma) is also contained within the inverted commas; no need for a capital letter after the reported speech – the word "said" simply continues the sentence; the start of the line (paragraph) is indented.

2 When the speech comes second:

The worried child said, "There was a huge fire in our road last night."

What to look out for: again, all the words spoken are contained within the inverted commas; the full stop at the end is contained within the inverted commas; a comma is used to separate the story from the speech (what else could you have used here, instead of a comma?); the start of the line (paragraph) is indented.

3 Mostly speech, a bit of narrative in between:

"There was a huge fire in our road last night," said the worried child, "and there were lots of fire engines!"

4 Other combinations of speech and narrative:

"There was a huge fire in our road last night," said the worried child, "and there were lots of fire engines! You could see the flames right up in the sky." Then she suddenly seemed to remember something important: "but nobody was hurt," she added.

5 When you have more than one speaker:

"There was a huge fire in our road last night," said the worried child, "and there were lots of fire engines!"

"What caused it?" asked his friends.

"I don't know. There are rumours about arson," he replied.

What to look out for: most importantly, notice that each new speaker is given a new line, indented, as each new line is a new paragraph.

Which to use, single (' ') or double (" ") inverted commas?

It is entirely up to you! But remember, whichever you choose, be consistent throughout a piece of work. You cannot vary between single and double – that would be very poor style.

USEFUL TERMS

There are a number of technical terms about language which are helpful in both reading and writing. In responses to reading – comprehensions, appreciations of literature, etc. you may need to use some of the terms, and they may also help you with your own writing. This list includes the basic **parts of speech**.

You will also be aware that you are marked in some sections of your exams for **knowledge about language**. This sometimes involves the use of technical terms to identify and describe features of language. The terms are listed alphabetically here:

Accent: see p51.

Acronym: an abbreviation, often instantly recognisable, usually formed from a combination of the first letters of a group of words. Sometimes acronyms are pronounced by their letters (AA, GCSE, RE, The UN, The USA, etc.), sometimes by a word that becomes formed by the first letters of the sequence of words (NATO), and sometimes by a combination of letters (OXFAM).

Adjective: a word used to describe or qualify a noun. Adjectives can express various features, e.g. quality (*big, small, rough, smooth*), quantity (*many, six*), distinguishing features (a *terraced* house, as opposed to a *detached* house).

Adverb: a word used to describe or qualify a verb. Adverbs often end in the letters *ly*. (He ran *quickly*, she walked *briskly*) – but there are many exceptions (He moved *sideways*, she ran *forward*, they were *often* late). Adverbs also serve the purpose of qualifying adjectives (He was *definitely* late, she was *beautifully* tanned),and other adverbs (She ran *extremely* quickly, he walked *very* slowly).

Alliteration: repetition of consonants, commonly used in poetry, to create an effect associated with meaning (*He spoke; the spirits from the sails descend* – "The Rape of the Lock", by Alexander Pope, l.137).

Ambiguity: double meanings – often writers deliberately want to suggest or imply more than one meaning in a phrase or word (*see also* irony).

Analogy: a comparison which does not use imagery – writers often describe a situation or event which is comparable to another one, the effect being that we can then understand the second situation more clearly (e.g. a story about tragic young love might be *analogous* to the story of *Romeo and Juliet*).

Argument essay: writing which presents points of view or opinion, usually backed up by facts and evidence.

Assonance: a combination of vowel sounds, commonly used in poetry, in order to add to the meaning (*The morning-dream that hover'd o'er her head* – "The Rape of the Lock", by Alexander Pope, l. 22).

Attitude: the outlook or point of view held by a writer.

Audience: now a commonly used term to mean "reader" – writers with a clear sense of audience are able to ask the key questions: who am I writing for and for what purpose? – they will then be able to use the most appropriate style, tone or register. The term is particularly useful if you are writing for a clear group of readers, e.g. a story for young children, a set of rules for school, a letter to the newspaper to complain about an issue. But it is not always a useful term – sometimes we just write for ourselves, or for a very general purpose, with no particular audience in mind.

Ballad: a poem that tells a story. Ballads often rhyme, and are frequently associated with traditional stories, sometimes based on legend, often derived from old folk tales with romantic, supernatural or other atmospheric settings.

Blank verse: unrhymed poetry.

Characterisation: how a writer will use language to build up and reveal characters (e.g. through speech, description of appearance, actions, etc.).

Clause: a distinct part of a sentence – as opposed to *phrases*, which are often just a few words. Clauses form units of meaning, like a sentence within a sentence, always with one main verb.

Cliché: a tired, habitually overworked phrase (see p5 for examples).

Colloquialisms: words or phrases which are informal, familiar, part of everyday speech, rather than appropriate in formal styles of writing – try to avoid colloquialisms in more formal writing, but you can use them to good effect, providing they fit the style, in more imaginative pieces.

Conjunction: a joining or linking word in a sentence (*and, or, but, because, if, though*, etc.).

Connotation: a word which carries with it a suggested or implied meaning – names of animals often hold connotations (pig, fish, snake, etc.) – that is, the words have come to hold associations for us other than just as animals.

Derivation: the origins of words.

Description: language used to create a picture of places, people, objects, moods, etc. – some might say that all parts of literature are, by their nature, descriptive, but some passages are brought more vividly to life by a writer's careful use of detail.

Dialect: see p51.

Dialogue: see p51, and note also how important speech is in literature to create characters.

Diction: the choice of words to give a particular slant to meanings – consider, for example, the differences suggested by these words: pupil/student; spectator/fan; storm/tempest.

Direct speech: speech reported in writing (see p8).

Drafting: the process of writing – early stages, through to refining ideas, then final copy, including proof-reading and editing.

Empathy: the ability of a writer to relate to an experience outside their own – to get into somebody else's mind or experiences; this is a skill commonly required in your writing at GCSE – frequently you are asked to take on the role of a particular character.

Evocation (evoke/evocative): the capacity of a writer to bring to life certain memories, feelings, associations – sometimes to call up a certain mood or atmosphere, or a sense of place.

Figurative language: non-literal use of language, often in the form of imagery, but sometimes as figures of speech, e.g. in sayings or proverbs (*a bird in the hand is worth two in the bush ... out of the frying pan, into the fire*).

Formal and **informal registers:** a formal register of language will be marked out by complete sentences, precise vocabulary, complex grammar, and an informal register might use colloquialisms, slang, shortened sentences, in writing which will seem more like conversation.

Genre: a type or collection of writing, e.g. romantic, realistic novel, gothic, fable, ballad, satire – the key thing is that to belong to a genre, a work will contain certain distinguishing features marking it out as a particular type of writing.

Grammar: the construction of language.

Hero: the principal character in a novel or play; usually to be a hero we expect the main character to be a decent sort of character, one who can be admired or held in high esteem.

Hyperbole: exaggeration – to coin a modern phrase, this is when writers "go over the top" with their use of language, suggesting that something is the strongest, the best, the greatest, which of course distorts the truth, (Here is another example from "The Rape of the Lock": *Belinda smiled, and all the world was gay.*).

Idiom: a phrase or expression in current use – often like colloquialisms, these will be familiar, or conversational, or even figurative (*Nice weather for the ducks ... She gave me a piece of her mind*).

Imagery: a non-literal contrast. There are three common types of images used: (examples are again taken from "The Rape of the Lock"):

> **Similes:**   *her eyes*
> *like the sun, shine on all alike*
> (a simile makes a comparison by stating that one thing is like another).

Metaphors: in another part of the poem, the writer refers to a pair of scissors:

> *The little engine on his fingers ends ...*

(a metaphor allows the object simply to become what it is being compared with, so in this case the scissors become the little engine, and there is no need for the writer to state that they are like the engine – in this way a metaphor is a more direct comparison).

Personification: this involves turning an object – either inanimate or from nature, into a human or animal form, with human or animal actions and feelings. Pope is here writing about the River Thames:

> *Thames with pride surveys his rising towers.*

It is essential to understand what is meant by *non-literal* language: eyes cannot literally be the sun; a pair of scissors cannot literally be an engine; a river cannot literally survey towers with pride!

Irony: irony is saying, or writing, one thing, and meaning another; think of it as a form of sarcasm – sometimes people are "put down", for example we might say "well done" to somebody who trips over some steps. Irony in literature is much the same, and is quite often intended to make fun of characters, reveal their weaknesses, or to mock them – so to find ironic language, look for hidden or double meanings.

Jargon: see p51.

Mood: often used nowadays to mean tone or atmosphere – you may be asked to describe the mood of some writing: is it sad, tragic, positive, optimistic, romantic, or what? Often you can see how mood has been created by analysing the use of adjectives and adverbs.

Narrator: the teller of a story; we often talk of "**the narrator's voice**" – who is telling the story?; does the teller of the story play a part in it?; is it written in the **first person**, or the **third person**, by the **omniscient narrator**? All of this makes up **narrative technique** – the ways in which a story is written.

Noun: that part of speech which is object (*knife*), thing (*gas*), place (*city*), abstraction (*happiness*), state (*death*), event (*game*), person (*mother*). **Proper nouns** are names or titles (*The Cup Final, John, London*, etc.).

Onomatopoeia: a word used to suggest its meaning by its sound – such as *crash* or *scream*, although clearly, in poetry, the effect will be less obvious, as in this, another example from "The Rape of the Lock":

> *Now lap-dogs give themselves the rousing shake.* (l.15)

Plot: the plan of events in a story or play – effectively the plot is what happens, as opposed to the subject or themes.

Pronoun: words such as *I, you, he, she, we, they, which, whose* – all words which replace nouns (or more accurately, which replace noun phrases).

Prose: the best way to define prose is to think of it as that writing which is *not* poetry; it is most commonly the writing in stories and novels, and will be characterised by the use of continuous sentences and paragraphs, but it is difficult to give a precise definition.

Pun: a play on words, involving double meanings, sometimes using homophones – words that sound the same, but with different meanings and perhaps different spellings. Shakespeare used a lot of these sorts of puns. *Julius Caesar* begins with a famous one: A citizen of Rome is asked what his job is, and he, a cobbler, jokingly replies that he is a "mender of bad *soles*" – can you see the pun, or double meaning, suggested by the sound of the word?

A lot of modern newspaper headlines are full of puns, often where there is an association of meanings between words: FAMOUS CRICKETER GIVEN BAIL … POLICEMAN JOINS BEAT GROUP … VICAR IS PREY OF LOCAL THUGS … think of your own!

Realism: writing which shows life as it really is – frequently writing which captures a sense of the truth, almost like a photograph or descriptive painting. The effect is often created by mention of down to earth objects, recognisable features, or dialogue which can almost be heard as if spoken aloud.

Register: an increasingly common term, used to mean the type of language being used in any particular situation; perhaps the best way to define register is by the word *variety* – possible different registers are: literary, poetic, formal, informal, lecture, discussion, informative, persuasive … but really the list is endless.

Rhetoric: nowadays we tend to use this term to mean persuasive, frequently elegant language, used in speeches and argument. Sometimes it is used as a way of criticising a speaker by implying that he has used words powerfully and convincingly, but without much substance in the argument. In the past, rhetoric more accurately meant "the art of speech-making".

Rhyme: words placed in a relationship in poetry, frequently at the ends of lines, due to their sounding the same, e.g.

> Behold, four kings in majesty *revered*,
> With hoary whiskers and a forky *beard*.   "The Rape of the Lock", l. 37-8.

Rhythm: the metre, or the beat of lines in poetry.

Satire: mockery in literature, intended to poke fun at characters, in order to expose their weaknesses, their foolishness, or their immorality; the best way to think of satire is to think of the popular television programme, *Spitting Image*.

Slang: see p51.

Standard English: the form of written and spoken English generally agreed as most appropriate for work, formal communications, business, education, journalism, etc.

Soliloquy: a speech in a play spoken by one character to the audience only – really a character thinking aloud; a technique used a great deal by Shakespeare.

Style: that part of literature which is to do with the expression, as opposed to the content, ideas, themes or subject matter – style is always associated with *how* literature is written rather than *what* it is about.

Symbol: the use of one thing to represent or suggest something else, in literature. We talk about objects or events being symbolic of a mood, feeling or idea, even if, at first glance they do not appear related.

Syntax: the way that sentences are constructed.

Themes: connected ideas which arise in literature, often revealed through the actions of more than one character, a number of events, or with features of the language which are expressed more than once – we might discover themes of love, fate, power, despair, innocence, evil, all to be interpreted from different parts of a work of literature. Some of the main themes in Shakespeare's plays would be: "Romeo and Juliet": *impatience*; "A Midsummer Night's Dream": *mischief*; "Julius Caesar": *honour*.

Tone: the overall mood or feeling of writing, for example the tone could be humorous, tragic, persuasive, mocking, serious, etc.

Verb: many young children are taught that verbs are "doing words", but this definition is now rejected as inadequate; more strictly, a verb is a "happening" or "occurring" word – the word(s) needed for something to take place in a sentence. Sentences cannot be formed without verbs, they would end up making no sense, as would be the case in the following example:

> The athlete *won* the race.

> Remove the verb, and see what you are left with:

> The athlete the race.

Vocabulary: the variety and selection of words; it is an important skill to extend your vocabulary, and the best way to do this is by using a thesaurus.

Voice: now a common term used to mean "the writer's sense of presence in a piece of writing" – you have probably been told by your teachers to "put something of yourself into your writing". This is achieved by being interested in what you have to say, so that there is evidence that you as a writer are genuinely expressing yourself.

Different writing tasks

This section aims to remind you of the range of **types of writing** that you need to be able to do in English exams. Writing is a very varied sort of activity. You need to be able to distinguish between the different demands of writing imaginatively, writing formally, writing to inform or to describe, writing personally, and writing for a particular audience.

There is also reference to **reading** and **understanding** skills in this section. It is, after all, very rare that we write without involving ourselves in reading, and responding to what we read. Try not to separate reading and writing in your mind. Think of one as dependent on the other.

A REPORT

Quite often you are given some information and then asked to write a report.

One of the most important things to do before starting to write your report is to ask yourself some questions. What am I writing this report for? Who am I writing this report for? Do I need to use all the information I have been given? Should I add ideas of my own?

What you are now going to read is some information. The task which follows is asking you to write a report.

STIMULUS MATERIAL

DISASTER

Some years ago a dreadful fire occurred at a London Underground station. It was the worst fire in the history of the London Underground. At 7.46p.m. on Wednesday November 18, 1987, a huge ball of flame shot from an escalator shaft across the booking hall at King's Cross Station. Thirty-one people died from the smoke and fire; six more were appallingly injured.

Piecing together the details, an official investigator's notebook contained the following:

FACT   escalators were made of wood/had been in service since 1939;
19.15   inspector in relevant area noticed no problem;
19.17   one man, peering through the gaps between escalator treads saw "a ball of sparks" moving with the escalator/he told the clerk/clerk reported it by telephone;
19.28   passenger pushed the emergency stop button at the top of the escalator/railman saw flames and put tape across the escalator to prevent passengers using it;
19.32   policeman made an alarm call over his radio;
19.36   flames and smoke had spread right across escalator/passengers took no notice – even stepping across the tape/police passed on alarm to fire service;
FACT   only one policeman on duty at ground level;
FACT   for a time trains continued to stop and discharge passengers;
FACT   no officials of the underground railway were on hand to advise;
FACT   passengers found one of the exit gates locked;
19.40   police officers at the foot of the escalators decided to ask for an instruction to be given to prevent trains stopping at the station;
19.42   first fire engines arrive at the station;
19.45   police started directing passengers up unaffected escalators;
19.46   explosion;
NOTE   cause of fire was probably a lighted match dropped onto accumulated dirt and grease under the escalator.

TASK

Using the details noted above, imagine you are the official investigator and write a report to the managing director of London Underground. You want to inform him of the facts but you may also wish to make some comments and recommendations.

What would the examiner have been expecting in this report? First of all some sense of audience would be expected – who was the report written for? The language should be businesslike, clear and not elaborate. For a report a heading is a sensible idea and certainly paragraphing should be clear; you might even divide it into clear sections with a heading for each section.

You should be careful to group facts together where this makes things clearer and think about the order in which you say things.

Clear recommendations are important here.

ANSWER

To the Managing Director London Underground Railway
Report on the fire at King's Cross Station – Wednesday November 18 1987

This report is focused on what I believe was the worst fire in the history of the London Underground. The result of the fire was that thirty one people died from the smoke and fire; six more were appallingly injured and thousands of pounds of damage was done.

The fire took place on the escalator shaft at King's Cross Station, where a fireball shot across the booking hall where many civilians were waiting for a train and collecting their tickets. The escalators were made of wood and had been in service since 1939, so were quite old. The wood caught a light very quickly and flames spread at quite a fast rate – should there have been an updated escalator system? The "ball of sparks" that appeared in the escalator was reported straight away by the clerk by telephone. It was efficiently done. At 19.28, a passenger then pushed the emergency stop button at the top of the escalator – railman saw the flames on escalator and for safety reasons put tape across the escalator.

Precautions were taken by the policemen but flames and smoke had spread right across escalator by 19.36. A lack of authority was shown by policemen and railstaff, as commuters stepped over safety tape. Fire service were called by the police at 19.36 to deal with fire.

Only one policeman had been on duty at ground level when the fire began. I believe that this is not enough to cope with an emergency. The trains were not stopped immediately from stopping at the station after the fire broke out, but continued to stop & discharge people – this was wrong as it endangered the passengers and crowded the area, making it increasingly hard to deal with the emergency services. There were also no officials of the underground railway on hand to advise people, so a lack of knowledge of the situation in hand was present.

The probable cause of the explosion, was a lighted match. I believe that a ban on smoking is also necessary.

N Ashton

15

A SUMMARY Summarising the information from a quite complicated piece of writing is an important skill to develop. We might at times choose to extract that information in note form, while at other times, we might be expected to write our own neat piece of coherent prose.

Printed below is an article which was printed in *The Times* on Monday February 21 1994. In it John Patten, who was then Secretary of State for Education, is talking about school league tables and the information which they give to the public. He clearly has a personal view that the league tables are valuable and he is clearly proud to have been associated with their introduction.

Your task, which is printed below the article, is not to express a view, but to extract the key facts from the article.

STIMULUS MATERIAL

Rising into another league

League tables are spurring our schools, says **John Patten**, Education Secretary

No doctor concerned to improve the health of a patient would prescribe a course of treatment or some surgery without checking that patient's vital signs. So it is with the health of our schools.

If standards are to be raised, we have to know how schools are performing. Unsubstantiated claims and anecdote do not allow us to see how a school is doing, nor do they tell us whether there has been any improvement. Without objective evidence, a course of treatment to improve performance cannot be prescribed. That is why we have published school performance tables, not without noise and tumult, since 1992. They are a vital diagnostic tool in gauging the health of our education system.

But I have come to believe that they are much more. They not only help to measure educational health, but they are actually improving the health of our schools. As such, they will, I believe, come to be seen as one of our most significant post-war educational innovations.

Of course, when we first published the tables, we were pilloried by our political opponents and by the educational "experts". They assured us that people did not want the tables, would not read them, would not be able to "understand" them and similar patronising claptrap; or that parents would make snap decisions about their child's future based on the tables alone.

I was not alone in knowing this to be élitist nonsense. Some of us firmly believed at the outset that parents wanted hard, objective information. We thought that they would use the tables sensibly to inform their choice of school, along with the other sources that we have made available, like school prospectuses and annual reports – as well as a dose of that invaluable ingredient, local gossip.

The row that erupted when I first published the tables has now happily subsided. The debate has switched to what should be *in* the tables. The tables are now accepted and are here to stay. They are important tools of accountability. The evidence is clear: parents have a right to know how their children's schools are performing and they *want* to know. In the last two years, demand for the tables has run at the rate of 1.2 million copies. Furthermore, newspapers have attempted to help to satisfy the insatiable appetite of their readers for this information by devoting enormous space to the tables.

When *The Sun* – with its acute nose for what a mass readership wants – publishes the tables, then that is excellent news. When the *Daily Mirror* starts, as it did in 1993, the game is surely won.

But the media coverage of the tables has been notable for its quality, as well as its quantity. The tables have provoked a fascinating debate about the successes and difficulties of our education system and perhaps taken us a step towards something this country has sadly – and to its cost – lacked: an education culture.

Last year, we expanded the tables by including vocational qualifications and the results of all independent schools, as well as reporting on levels of school truancy. We also introduced new tables on further education and sixth-form college results. Today, I have announced plans for this year's tables. Information on levels of truancy – which last year helped to flush out one of this country's hidden problems – will be developed and refined to include both authorised and unauthorised absences. And we will report for the first time on the number of hours taught by each school, following the startling revelation by the schools' watchdog, Ofsted, that some children are being denied the equivalent of one year in five of their education.

So schools performance tables are here to stay. For they not only serve an important diagnostic purpose – taking and reporting on the education temperature of a school – but they are also vital in helping to improve its intellectual fitness. They help to drive up standards. They energise schools to examine their performance. They thus have an irreversible educational ratchet effect. Schools can compare their performance with other schools but, equally if not more importantly, they can compare it with their own performance over time. They can thus test the extent to which they have added some value. Schools which have higher expectations of their pupils will get more in return. If there is alas no improvement, they might need to introduce a new course of treatment. And that is just what many school management teams have started to do.

Take the Cumberland School in Newham, for example, whose performance in the 1992 tables inspired it to set up an action plan to improve results. By the time of the publication of the 1993 tables, the plan was already bearing fruit. Or the Nicholas School in Basildon, which was similarly spurred on by its showing in the tables. It identified strategies for improvements, such as a monitoring system for GCSE students and supervised study sessions after school. Results in five-plus A-C GCSEs rose from 5 per cent in 1992 to 17 per cent in 1993.

Some people say that so-called "raw" figures may distort what schools actually achieve: the seemingly modest results of a school in a more difficult area may be much more creditable than the good results of a school with a different ability intake. I have some sympathy with this argument. Hardworking pupils and teachers deserve proper recognition. But I have also seen for myself enough examples of schools in difficult areas, outperforming not just the local but the national average, to persuade me that results should not be adjusted to reflect in some way or other the supposed social and educational background of a school's intake; this is fiendishly hard to measure in any event. Real value-added measures – how much, say, pupils aged 11 improve in a particular school up to the age of 16 – will be extremely valuable and we are working towards that.

But equally we should never forget that "raw" data – *viz* exam results – are the educational currency young people carry in their pockets as they launch themselves in their careers.

Those who monotonously criticise the publication of results as unfair should look upon the tables as an opportunity, not a threat. The self esteem of a school is not threatened by its position in the tables alone, but more by a failure to improve itself. Conversely, the potential to use the information to positive effect stares us in the face.

Exam results are not the be-all and end-all of what school is about. But they are a vital indicator, to both parents and pupils. They are the equivalent of a health test, to show an intending employer that a person is fully fit for the job.

Let us be in no doubt. There can be no going back on putting exam results in the public domain. Without having results publicly available, some schools could relapse into complacency, thinking they are performing better than comparable schools. They can delude themselves that they are in a much healthier state than they are. That way lies the educational equivalent of arterial sclerosis.

Better they know how they are doing now and respond accordingly. In the end we should not be in the business of keeping any school on a life support machine. On the other had, we want to be able to breathe new life into those schools which have the ability to recover. To them, the performance tables should be seen as a challenge to be risen to, not a death warrant waiting to be signed.

Summarise, in about 250 words, the main points from the passage.

Examiner's tip
The passage in the newspaper is in fact a speech given by John Patten and is written in the first person. You should write your summary in the third person, that is using "he" and "they" rather than "I" and "we".

The task which you have been given contains only one significant word which you must interpret and that is the word "main". You must exercise your judgement and determine which are the main points being made in the passage, which are important and which are unimportant or even trivial. Make sure that you read the article several times while making your preliminary notes and make sure you really do ask yourself the question, "What is most important?" For instance, is what is said about *The Sun* and *The Daily Mirror* important?

One other thing about the task is that it suggests a number of words for you to use. You will find quite frequently that examination questions contain a suggestion of the length of the answer. It is important, though, that you do not waste time counting words. During your preparation spend a little time writing a passage of 100, 200, 250, 300 words in your normal handwriting so that you come to know without counting what these amounts look like in your writing. That preparation will mean no time wasted in the examination.

Rising into another *league*

In order to raise the standards of schools, we need objective evidence to examine their performance.

As with everything there has been opposition to the tables. Educational experts claimed that parents would not fully understand what they were for, and make rash judgements on where to send their children on them alone.

This debate has now changed to what should be in the tables. Demand for the tables has increased, and more and more newspapers are supplying for this demand.

The tables are being increased to include not simply academic results, but important issues such as levels of *truancy*. The tables are exposing problems that have previously been covered up.

Schools are now being able to compare themselves to others, and to make certain that there is room for improvement. Schools which begin to expect more from its pupils generally find that they get more in return. The result of this has been a rise in A–C GCSE results from 5% in 1992 to 17% in 1993.

However these results could fail to identify the true achievement of a school, especially one from a difficult area. But improvement in the tables can be clearly seen, softening this argument.

The tables are set out as an opportunity, not a threat. The public wants to know results, and by printing them we are encouraging schools to continue improving themselves and striving for the best possible results.

This is a secure summary, containing a couple of spelling errors, but generally well written.

You are sometimes given some information and then asked to write a speech. You must look at this information carefully as it is important to use all the material when you are putting the speech together. You must also look at the task carefully as you will be told who you will be writing the speech for, and this will affect the style of your writing.

What you are going to read now is an article which was published in *The Coventry Evening Telegraph* under the headline "The creepy subject of Darren's collecting bug".

The creepy subject of Darren's collecting bug

The day Darren Mann left primary school his teacher presented him with a parting gift – four hissing cockroaches. It was a wonderful present, he recalls. They make lovely pets.

It's very much a minority view. Few creepy crawlies have a poorer public image than the humble cockroach. Associated with poor hygiene and the spread of disease, it's a target for extermination wherever it raises its ugly head.

But it has a passionate defender in Darren Mann, and at 22 the former student is rapidly becoming a British authority on the insect most people love to hate.

Five years ago he started a cockroach study group with members all over the world.

Although Darren is employed by a Nature Conservation Trust, he is temporarily working at a museum, and he's also official recorder for all species found in his locality.

He keeps about two thousand of the little beasts in a garden shed at the family home, where he spends hours every day feeding them sliced apple and specialist food produced for pet rats. He likes nothing better than to put his hand into a squirming tankful and let them tickle his fingers.

The very thought makes environmental health officer George Makin cringe. He says that the common cockroach is rapidly moving up the public enemy list. He has recently had to close down several food premises and has no hesitation in describing the cockroach as a health hazard, a carrier of diseases like salmonella that must be rooted out and eradicated wherever it is found.

That's by no means easy. Cockroaches are among the great survivors of the animal kingdom. They'll eat almost anything, including each other and the paste used to stick on wallpaper, and they can live in the tiniest crack in a skirting board.

There are insecticides that will kill them, but spraying has to be a repetitive and time-consuming business. Miss one clutch of eggs, laid in profusion and protected with a hardened case, and the tribe will return.

Treat one apartment in a tower block, or a single house in a row, to get rid of them and they will simply move on to the next. However, Geoff Makin says that the scale of the problem in homes in the area for which he is responsible seems relatively small. But Darren Mann is not so sure.

'I think the stigma may be preventing people from reporting cockroaches. If you say you have them in your home people think you are poor. Yet that's wrong. I know a luxury apartment that has loads of them.'

Darren believes cockroaches are being unfairly maligned. He's not convinced that they are a major cause of the spread of salmonella and he says that it's their lifestyle, scuttling far and wide in search of food under cover of darkness, that makes them unloved.

Despite the dirty brown appearance of the British cockroach, all cockroaches actually spend almost half their waking moments cleaning themselves, he reveals.

It is the creature's ability to live on the margins, cleverly exploiting opportunities, that excites Darren's admiration. For years he's been exchanging live specimens through the

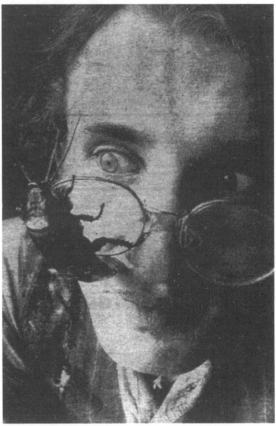

Seeing eye to eye: *Darren Mann with one of his Madagascan hissing cockroaches*

post with fellow enthusiasts. He didn't realise the practice had been made illegal until a recent batch was returned with a stiff warning. The collection in his shed numbers many species from abroad, some of them clothed in metallic purples and greens, a far cry from the dirty brown insects widely regarded as pests.

His problem now is keeping down the numbers of the commoner species. A single pair can reproduce themselves at a fantastic pace and the collection, housed in forty fish tanks, had to be moved into the shed after outgrowing his parents' house.

They're quite happy about several thousand cockroaches living at the bottom of the garden. And Darren's girlfirend takes it in her stride too. 'She thinks they're quite cute actually,' he says, 'although she tends to scratch a bit when she comes out of the shed.'

As an insect collector who can't pass a stone without lifting it to see what's underneath, Darren is about to broaden his horizons.

Next month he's off to Madagascar with a party of fellow enthusiasts to study some of the more exotic species of cockroach in their natural habitat. He's itching to get there.

Imagine that you are Darren and that you have been asked to make a speech to a public meeting of the local branch of the Nature Conservation Trust about cockroaches. Write your speech.

UCLES 1993

TASK

Examiner's tip   There is a lot of information in the article which should be used. Points should be considered and careful thought given to their order for best effect. The speech should also be written in a style suitable for Darren, e.g. he might be thought to sound rather eccentric. Consideration should be given to conveying his character through the way he speaks.

It is probable that Darren's audience would not all be as fascinated by cockroaches as he is and, as well as giving information, Darren would be trying to be persuasive in what he is saying.

Humour would probably not be a bad idea either!

In short, the material is not particularly difficult to tease out to use but what is crucial in the answer is that the style must be right.

ANSWER

The creepy subject of Darren's collecting bug.

The day I left primary school, my teacher gave me the best present I have ever had — my first few cockroaches. These soon multiplied to the number I have now, this being about 2000. They are easy pets to keep, and feeding consists of sliced apple, and food which can be obtained from pet stores catering for pet rats.

For 5 years we have had a small group from all over the world, studying cockroaches.

Of course most of you will associate the cockroach with being a health hazard and a pest. It is true that many food establishments will be closed down if cockroaches are found in them, but I am still not convinced that they are carriers of such diseases as salmonella, at least not the main carriers. I am constantly amazed at how great cockroaches are at surviving. Maybe we should take a leaf out of their book. They will eat anything, wallpaper paste, and even each other in order to survive. The reason that people feel threatened by them is that they do travel so far, and reproduce so quickly, but there is nothing to be ashamed of in having cockroaches in your house. We honestly do not believe that you have the most unclean house in England if you are occupied by cockroaches. After all, they wouldn't want to live there themselves if it was completely disgusting!

I did used to have quite a regular collectors club going on, unfortunately I did not realize that it was illegal to send cockroaches through the post. But that just goes to show how versatile the little things are, they didn't mind at all, it was just the royal mail who protested!

If my parents can cope with 2000 cockroaches in their garden shed, and my girlfriend thinks that they are quite cute, then I don't see why the general public can't learn to live with them and love them as pets.

Some of the foreign species are the most amazing colours, and next month, myself and some fellow enthusiasts shall be off to Madagascar to study some more of these exotic species. And as many people are itching to get rid of them, I am itching to get at them.

Letts
Q&A

A LETTER

Essentially there are two types of letter which you might be asked to write in an examination. The first is a formal letter and the second a personal letter.

There are differences in the style and layout but in these days of word processing, desk-top publishing and generally improving technology, it is no longer possible to say that there is one right way to lay out a letter and that other ways are wrong.

What we can say is that if you are writing a formal letter it should be headed with your address and the name and address of the person who is to receive the letter. It should be dated and the recipient should be addressed either by name or by a title, "Sir" or "Madam". If you use a name then end the letter "Yours sincerely"; if you use a title then end the letter "Yours faithfully". A most important thing is that your letter looks neat and professional.

If you are writing a personal letter you should put your own address and the date but there is no need to put the recipient's name and address. You may choose to end the letter with "Yours sincerely" but you may also choose to end it more informally.

Below is some information about cigarettes and passive smoking which is taken from a book called *The Environment and Health*. The task, a letter-writing task, follows.

STIMULUS MATERIAL

Cigarettes and passive smoking

Nearly everyone now accepts that cigarette smoking greatly increases the risk of bronchitis, lung cancer or heart disease. But around a third of the adult population continues to smoke, and many young people take up the habit.

Unfortunately, cigarette smoking does not only affect the smoker; it damages the environment and the health of other people too. Just being in a smoky room is the equivalent of smoking one cigarette for every 20 actually being smoked.

There is now no doubt that exposure to other people's cigarette smoke is damaging to health. Lung cancer is more common than usual in non-smokers who work in smoky environments. Children whose parents smoke are more likely to suffer from coughs and respiratory diseases.

Many smokers are not aware of the irritation their habit can cause to non-smokers. Children often grow up in a smoky environment, which can damage their lungs from an early age.

The risk seems to be greatest for the families of smokers, and young people are more likely to suffer lung problems if their parents smoke. It is known that the non-smoking wives of male smokers are about a third more likely to develop lung cancer than the non-smoking wives of non-smokers. The smoke drifting from another person's cigarette contains a much worse mixture of damaging chemicals than the smoke the smoker inhales – five times as much carbon monoxide, which can be harmful to the heart and circulation, and about fifty times as much of the cancer-causing chemicals.

Respiratory illness 5–9 years

Persistent cough 8–19 years

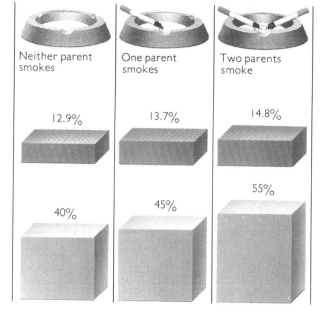

Neither parent smokes — 12.9% — 40%

One parent smokes — 13.7% — 45%

Two parents smoke — 14.8% — 55%

TASK

You have a friend who smokes and you are anxious that they should give up because you believe they are damaging their health. Write a persuasive letter to your friend in which you try to convince her/him that not smoking is better. Use information from the stimulus material to help you form your argument.

TASK

Examiner's tip As is so often the case there is a key word here in the task which you must recognise. The word is "persuasive". This should set the tone for the answer. You might start and end the letter in a friendly, informal manner, but the key purpose is to offer clear advice. You are writing with a serious purpose in mind and that purpose is to persuade your friend to give up smoking.

Make sure then that you get the tone right; friendly but sincere and genuine in your concern.

Use points from the information given but add points of your own. (It might be a help if you are able to think of a real friend when you are working out what to say and what the reaction is likely to be when the letter is received.)

ANSWER

> 69. Broome Manor Lane
> Swindon
> Wilts.
> SN3 1NB.
> 31st. July, 1994.
>
> Dear Nicky,
>   How's it going? Hope you are well — considering the amount you smoke each day! No, I'm not going to lecture, but I am concerned about your smoking habit, especially when you look at the statistics. I just don't understand why you do it when you see your mum with her bronchitis, from smoking for however many years. And you may not be lucky enough to get just bronchitis, you could get lung cancer, or some kind of heart disease. Is that really worth it just to look cool in front of the older guys? And have you ever thought about what you are doing to me. I have to sit there breathing in your smoke for hours on end, I'm just glad I'm not married to you! The other day I found out that the smoke I accidently inhale from your cigarettes contains far more damaging chemicals than the smoke that is going inside of you. So if I end up with cancer then I'll know who to blame.
>   But, I can't force you to stop, just think about smoking in other peoples company, especially children. You don't want the increase in children having lung cancer on your conscience now do you?
>   Anyway, lecture over, take care and write back soon.
>
>   love
>   Becky

A NARRATIVE

You are sometimes asked to write a narrative, possibly a story. You might just be given a title which you are free to interpret in any way you like. You might be given an extract of narrative writing to give you ideas for your own writing.

In this case, before getting down to your writing, you should think of what you have discovered about the two characters, what might happen which is consistent with what you have learnt about the characters, and what you should do to copy Ewan Clarkson's style of writing.

What you are going to read now is an extract from a novel. The task which follows asks you to write in a narrative style.

STIMULUS MATERIAL

ICE TREK by EWAN CLARKSON

(Two very different men are stranded together after a plane crash)

Suddenly Larsen remembered his knife. It was the sort of penknife beloved of small boys, no more than a toy, an intricate maze of folding blades and gadgets, all wholly impractical but delightfully ingenious. He produced it for Umiak's inspection.

He had expected ridicule. Instead Umiak stared at it intently, and then began a prolonged and meticulous examination, testing every blade and gadget, opening and closing each one several times.

They found a use for it straight away, converting the gallon can into a petrol stove, using dry sand from beside the stream. Together they designed it, cutting a flap of metal from one side of the can, but leaving it hinged to act as a windshield or perhaps, they hoped, a hot-plate. They had trouble draining petrol from the fuel tank of the plane but at last they had about half a gallon in a plastic bag. The fire burned well but, to Larsen's chagrin, with a sooty black flame which Umiak explained was caused by sea oil from the can. Umiak suggested a drink of hot water but Larsen remained frustrated as there appeared to be nothing to boil it in.

Umiak sat silent for a while. Then he got up and began pottering among the stones. Larsen sat on alone, hunched over the flames of the stove, straining his ears in the hope of hearing a plane. There was nothing, no sound save that of Umiak clattering among the rocks. The valley was devoid of life, and not even a raven showed in the sky above the crags.

His reverie was interrupted by Umiak, who appeared at his side with a handful of round flat pebbles, which he proceeded to pile on the stove. Then he squatted back on his heels, watching the flames play over the stones. Nearby he had built a nest of rocks and moss, lining it with a plastic bag which he had half filled with water. When he judged the pebbles hot enough he deftly shovelled them out of the flames, using two flat slates he had chosen for the purpose. Swiftly he transferred them to the water, which hissed and bubbled as the stones sank. In a few moments the water was too hot to touch.

Umiak dipped the cup in the water and offered it to Larsen. The brew did not look inviting. The stones had blackened with carbon from the residue of the seal oil, and bits of it had floated on the surface. Despite Umiak's insistence Larsen was not tempted. He was tired of lessons in survival and Umiak, sensing this, drained the cup and then sat silent. The white man depressed him. Umiak wandered down the valley. Alone he knew he could survive, and this knowledge, blended with an instinctive love of the land of which he felt so much a part, left no room in his mind for fear or concern.

The presence of the white man did though. There was a fundamental difference between the two races, in their attitude to the world around them. For ten thousand years his people had learned to live with the land, and to make the best use of all it had to offer. At some point during that time the white men, the strangers, had chosen not to adapt their ways to natural cycles, and instead had learned to domesticate stock and to cultivate crops. From that point on they had been compelled more and more to fight against the forces of the wild.

In the days to come Larsen would grow to need him. The man was not yet prepared to accept this, and Umiak was not sure how to convince him without antagonising him. On the other hand he did not need Larsen.

"In the days to come Larsen would grow to need him." Write a continuation which shows what you think did happen.

TASK

UCLES 1993

Examiner's tip   One thing which is essential here is that you really get into the extract and understand the characters. Larsen and Umiak are very different having been raised in different cultures and Umiak clearly stands a far better chance of coping than Larsen.

Their relationship could clearly develop at one of two extremes, complete antagonism or mutual trust; or the development could be somewhere in between. You must decide what is most likely.

Do not forget to use the passage. In considering what is likely to happen you must consider what has already happened as your writing must be a logical progression.

You must also consider the style in which the extract is written. You have been asked to write a continuation and you should therefore be making an attempt to write in the same style. You should, for instance, look at the type of vocabulary which has been used. You might also look at the sentence structure; for instance many of the sentences in the extract are quite short and succinct and there are few long complex sentences.

ANSWER

Shahzad Hussain.

STAR TREK

– CONTINUATION

In the days to come Larsen would grow to need him. Umiak knew that he himself could survive until help arrived but Larsen on his own had no chance of survival.

Later on Umiak decided to put a proposal to Larsen saying that Larsen would cooperate with Umiak or they would go their own separate ways. Larsen somewhat surprised at Umiak's proposal, hastily agreed to cooperate.

Just by the sound of his voice Umiak knew that Larsen was not prepared to do anything. Larsen just sitting there fiddling with his penknife depressed Umiak. Umiak snatched the knife out of his hands and took it inside the wreckage. Larsen intrigued by this immediately got up and followed Umiak inside the remains of the plane. There he saw Umiak with his knife cutting off the foam and sponge of the chair. Larsen seeing this stopped and realised what a fool he had been degrading Umiak and thinking of him as the lower human being. He was a sea of knowledge, boiling water with rocks and a plastic bag. His knowledge was vital for survival. One way or another he would have to cooperate.

Then after his long thoughts, Larsen immediately proceeded towards Umiak and seeing Umiak feeling tired and weary took the knife from his hands and started collecting the foam and sponge. Umiak observing this felt a great sense of relief and a smile appeared across his face.

After a little while, Umiak and Larsen taking turns to collect the sponge, had a great big heap of sponge. They together went round the wreckage seeing the best place for shelter. It seemed as though their differences had all of a sudden had been resolved.

Umiak started to bring the sponge to the appointed place and spreading evenly the sponge among the ground. A good friendship was about to start. Well written with a nice pace –
NEW CHAPTER. Well done (A)

23

Responding to different kinds of stimulus material

This section is all about "responding to stimuli" – or, put more simply, doing the tasks set. It is divided into three parts: Comprehension, Literary stimulus and Media stimulus. Within each of these parts you will find detailed examination tasks (or questions) with some examples of responses (or answers) written by real pupils.

If you really want a challenge, why not have a go at the tasks yourself before you look at the responses of the pupils?

At the end of the section see if you have been able to identify the main principles involved in responding to English exam questions. In English you are never marked for getting answers right or wrong. Using and understanding English – your own language – can never be as simple as that. So try to use this section to grasp what sorts of things you will be marked for.

COMPREHENSION

Comprehension is a general word which means "understanding". In exams you are asked to read passages, and to show that you understand them you are then asked a series of questions about the meanings and language.

It is important that you understand some of the skills involved in answering comprehension questions; what is most important is that you learn how to interpret the types of questions that you are asked.

First, let's look at a comprehension passage and the answers that have been written by one pupil. Read the following passage carefully and then answer the questions that follow. You should try to answer all the questions and, as far as possible, to answer in your own words.

The writer, a travel writer, Michael Palin, is recounting a journey from the North to South Poles. Near the start of his journey, he and his group of travellers are on Day 6, and have reached Kap Wik which is still in the far north. The passage describes his reception at the home of Harald Solheim, who lives near the Arctic Circle.

STIMULUS MATERIAL

DAY 6 KAP WIK TO LONGYEARBYEN

It's 2.45 in the morning when we arrive at Harald Solheim's hut. A tall wooden frame hung with seal carcasses stands on a slight rise, more prominent than the cabin itself, which is set lower down, out of the wind. The first surprise is Harald himself. Instead of some grizzly bearded old-timer, a tall, pale, studious figure comes out to welcome us. He does have a beard, but attached as it is to long, aquiline features the effect is more rabbi than trapper. The second surprise is how benignly and agreeably he copes with the appearance of ten tired and hungry travellers in the middle of the night. First we fill up his miniscule hallway with our boots and bags, then we burst his sitting-room to the seams, whilst he heats up some stew on a wood-burning stove. His wood supply, neatly stacked in a workshop, is driftwood, probably from the Russian coast. His electricity supply is wind-generated.

He fetches out a leg of smoked reindeer which is quite delicious and over this and a mixture of stew, smoked salmon, Aquavit (the local spirit) and Glenmorangie whisky we thaw out and swap stories. Harald offers advice, comment and information, liberally laced with dry humour. It's like some wonderfully chaotic tutorial.

Around about 4.30 a.m. some of us start looking a little anxiously for the dormitory. Harald explains the arrangements. In a next-door room he has four bunk-beds and floor space for two. There is more space on the floor of his workshop. Everyone else will have to sleep in the sitting-room with him. There is one sit-down loo, but as this is a bag that has to be emptied men are requested to use the Great Outdoors whenever possible, but to refrain from peeing on the side

of the house from which he draws his water supply. For cleaning teeth and washing he recommends the snow.

When I wake, it's half-past eleven. The sitting-room resembles some Viking Valhalla with recumbent Norwegians scattered about and Harald sprawled on the sofa like a warrior slain in battle. Then the telephone rings. Last night my tired brain was so busy romanticizing Harald's existence that I hadn't noticed the phone, or the remote control for the matt-black hi-fi, or the visitor's book, or the collection of Rachmaninov piano concertos on CD, signed 'To Harald from Vladimir Askenazy'. Is it all a dream? Have we been hi-jacked in the night to some apartment in Oslo? I stumble outside clutching my toothbrush and there is the reassuring reality of empty mountains and frozen seas stretching as far as the eye can see.

I scrub snow all over my face and neck. A refreshing shock which dispels any lurking hangover. When I get back indoors Harald is off the phone and preparing coffee. This autumn, he tells me, he will be celebrating 15 years at Kap Wik. He has family in Norway, but they don't visit much. His closest neighbours are the Russians at the mining town of Pyramiden, 18 miles away. He reads a lot, 'Almost everything except religious literature' and hunts seal, reindeer, Arctic fox (a pelt will fetch around £80) and snowgeese, ' "Goose Kap Wik" was served to the King and Queen of Norway,' he informs me, with quiet satisfaction.

'So it's a busy life in the middle of nowhere?'

Harald shrugs. 'Some years I don't see a living soul from autumn to July.'

I ask him if he has ever felt the need for companionship. A woman around the house perhaps.

'It's… er…,' he smiles at his sudden inarticulacy… 'it's not easy to explain in Norwegian… but any woman mad enough to come here…'

He never finishes the sentence. The sound of a distant helicopter brings him to his feet.

'It's my mail', he explains, almost apologetically, as a Sea King helicopter clatters into sight across the fiord.

After a late lunch and more stories our caravan is repacked and relaunched. Harald, smiling, waves us away. I don't really understand why a man of such curiosity, fluency and culture should want to chase animals around Spitsbergen, but I feel he rather enjoys being an enigma, and though he is no hermit he is one of a rare breed of truly independent men.

The rest of the journey is less eventful. The slopes are not as fierce, and the snow is turning to slush in some of the valleys. It's becoming almost routine to turn off one glacier onto another, to roar up snowbound mountain passes and see the seals plop back into their ice-holes as we cross the fiords.

We stop for a while at the spot where Patti had an adventure on the way up to Ny Alesund. She lost her way in a 'white-out' and was not found for almost an hour. I hope this isn't an omen for the long journey ahead.

Although we make fast progress towards Longyearbyen, the weather has not finished with us. Turning into the broad valley that leads to the town we are hit full in the face by a blizzard of stinging wet snow and as Heinrich accelerates for home it makes for a hard and uncomfortable end to the ride.

After five and a half hours travelling we see through the murk the first lights of Longyearbyen, and the snowmobiles screech clumsily along the wet highway.

It's half-past ten and we have reached our first town, 812 miles from the North Pole.

QUESTIONS

1 In the writing, there is a lot of evidence of the type of life that Harald lived. Describe his way of life, giving examples of the evidence available in the passage.

2 The writer uses a variety of detail to give an impression of Harald's character. Show how his character is created through:
- physical description;
- the account of Harald's relations with the group of travellers;
- the account of his possessions;
- his attitude to life.

3 How successfully has the writer used language to describe the scene and to create the mood and atmosphere of the place?

4 In your own words explain the meanings of the words and phrases printed below in bold type:

"The second surprise is **how benignly and agreeably** he copes with the appearance of ten tired and hungry travellers in the middle of the night."

"Harald offers advice, comment and information, **liberally laced with dry humour**."

"… but I feel he rather enjoys **being an enigma**."

5 This extract describes one small part of the writer's journey. What are the features in the writing that would make you interested in following the story of the rest of the journey?

ANSWERS

Here are a pupil's answers to the comprehension questions. As you are reading them, try to ask yourself these questions, which are about the skills used:
- Has he shown understanding of the passage?
- Has he been able to select relevant parts of the passage to answer the questions precisely?
- Has he supported his answers with adequate evidence, through close reference to examples in the writing?
- Does his own written expression help to get across his meanings?

To save you from looking back at the questions on each occasion, these are repeated for you at the start of each answer:

1 In the writing, there is a lot of evidence of the type of life that Harald lived. Describe his way of life, giving examples of the evidence available in the passage.

> 1. Harold lives in an isolated place. He lives an almost solitary existence, only seeing a few people a year. ("Some years I don't see anyone from Autumn to July.") He lives off the food he can hunt from around the mountians and valleys where he lives. As he is further north than the most northern towns he suffers greatly from the cold. He hunts the animals that live in this area; seals, reindeer, salmon, and does quite well from them. As well as living quite a remote and basic life, which is shown because he has no proper toilet and collects his water from the roof of his house, he also has quite a morden furnished home with plenty of comforts,

having things like a remote controlled hi-fi, telephone and large numbers of CD's. He has quite good links to other people. He has his post delivered by a helicopter and he has his phone, but if he had an accident outside the house he probably wouldn't be able to receive any outside assistance.

He has taken advantage of the area he lives in to help equip his home and to help him live. This is shown in the way his wood supply is probably driftwood from the Russian coast and his electricity supply is wind-generated.

Even though Harold's life is one of loneliness, he welcomes visitors with great hospitality. This is shown by the way that he offers good food, Aquavit, and whisky. His way of life is also quite cultured, as he listens to Rachmaninov piano concertos on CD. As well as listening to music, he also seems to have a life where he is a constant reader, perhaps this is to stimulate his mind as he is on his own for the majority of the time.

Examiner's commentary

In this answer the pupil has used a variety of points to show different features of his way of life. Clearly he has gone through the passage and identified the main points. These take account of Harald's surroundings and the way he treats his visitors. Thus, there is good use of the evidence.

2 The writer uses a variety of detail to give an impression of Harald's character. Show how his character is created through:

- physical description;
- the account of Harald's relations with the group of travellers;
- the account of his possessions;
- his attitude to life.

2. When the party reaches Harold's hut it is obvious the author is expecting a very rugged, burly man with a beard, tangled hair and weathered skin. Harold, however, is not the man of the image in the author's mind. He turns out to be "a tall, pale, studious figure." This, plus his rabbi beard, seems to show him to be educated and quite sophisticated.

ANSWERS

His reactions to the appearance of the travellers, in the middle of the night, is genial, with an even temper. They were expecting a stereotype of the local people, rugged and grizzly, but instead he is kind and friendly ("how benignly and agreably he copes with the appearance of ten tired and hungry travellers"). Also, the way he relates to his guests, by listening to and entertaining them, proves him to be an excellent host. Once the party has sat down, to a meal that Harold has prepared, Harold is described as giving "advice, comment and information, liberally laced with dry humour." This might mean that he has a good relationship with the travellers, he can set up an instant friendship, by making himself very popular. But in the way he treats these strangers in his home, it is like he has known them all his life, so he is trusting, and doesn't expect them to do any wrong.

His possessions show him to be a well-educated and modern man with a lot of time to kill. I think although Harold does like and enjoy the outdoors, he also likes the comfort of his own home and he likes some luxuries, but when you think that he possesses up to date facilities like the CDs and the phone, as well as the books, then these may suggest that he is lonely because he cannot relate to or communicate to other people a lot.

His attitude to life coupled with his chosen place of residence makes him seem something of a loner, but completely independent and in control of his own life.

3 How successfully has the writer used language to describe the scene and to create the mood and atmosphere of the place?

3. I think the writer has been quite successful in his use of description. Much of the description is quite concise, but the adjectives used are in order to help us create a clear picture in our minds, eg "grizzly bearded."

The scene at first seems very primitive, which is shown through description of 'A tall wooden frame hung with seal carcasses,' and the use of the word 'hut' seems in keeping with the archaic scene. This illusion is shattered by the eloquence and humour of the educated dweller's speech.

The atmosphere is one of desolation, portrayed by the picture of "empty mountains" and the way that the helicopter "clatters" into sight. Also, the time of day helps me to create the mood, and then the primitive feeling returns in the description of the toilet and washing facilities, which involve snow, a small bag and a toothbrush. This theme is carried through in a description of the sitting rooms as a "Viking Valhalla" and in the image of Harold as a "warrior slain in battle." This primitive, Northern Viking impression is changed by the presence of the modern conveniences, but the desolation returns when Harold says that some years he sees no-one for six months and that his nearest neighbour lives eighteen miles away. Altogether, the lonely mood is helped by the friendly atmosphere created when Harold has company. One other thing you notice is that it is all written in the present tense, which makes the action feel as if it is happening.

Examiner's commentary

This is a successful answer particularly in the way that the pupil has shown how the atmosphere is created. There are sufficient references to the techniques of language used.

4 In your own words explain the meanings of the words and phrases printed below in bold type:

"The second surprise is how **benignly and agreeably** he copes with the appearance of ten tired and hungry travellers in the middle of the night."

This means that he welcomed the travellers warmly, in a friendly way. He was calm and settling, reassuring towards the ten of them.

"Harald offers advice, comment and information, **liberally laced with dry humour**."

This means that his advice, comments and information always have a bit of wit in them, like a joke to keep the listener interested in what was said.

29

ANSWERS

"… but I feel he rather enjoys **being an enigma**."

> He liked to be a man of contradictions. He kept
> things secret, and so he was not easy to understand.

Examiner's commentary

The pupil has understood the vocabulary and been able to explain the meanings concisely.

5   This extract describes one small part of the writer's journey. What are the features in the writing that would make you interested in following the story of the rest of the journey?

> 5. I found this passage very interesting and I personally would enjoy reading on. I become interested in the adventures, problems and discoveries that the travellers will make on their journey. I get the impression that if I do read on, the interest will be kept up by the detailed description about his surroundings, and especially about the characters who he comes across. At the end of this extract, I feel that I have got to know Harold, and I predict that there will be many more people who will be described just as well so that I will get to know them just as if I was on the journey too.
>
> Harold's life seems one of repetitiveness: no opportunities crop up each day, few distractions of other humans, very cut off from the outside world. His life will carry on all the time, the door always open as a welcoming sight for all weary travellers passing through his route. I get the feeling that there will be lots more people in other parts of the world and so we will get variety of people in the book. This is what makes me want to read on.

Examiner's commentary

These questions are always difficult because they are so open-ended. This pupil has answered the question well. His reasons for wanting to read on are relevant to the strengths of the passage. He makes points about the qualities of the passage, particularly the way that it deals with understanding of an unusual lifestyle. This is preferable to statements which simply say "I like the passage", or "I would like to read on because it was interesting."

What you will find printed on the next few pages is some material from literature. The first is from a book called *This Time Next Week* by Leslie Thomas, and the second is a poem called *A Moment of Respect* by Edwin Brock.

Material from literature is used for a variety of reasons. Sometimes you are asked to examine the language which may be particularly descriptive or evocative. Sometimes, as in this case, you may be asked to examine the characters and relationships, to comment on them and to explore similar kinds of characterisation yourself.

THIS TIME NEXT WEEK, by Leslie Thomas.

EVERY NOW AND then my father would blow home from sea and break a few windows. He used to smash the windows, generally at the front of the house, because my mother would not let him in. She said they were legally separated and nothing was going to change it.

One day the mistress of the cub pack to which I belonged came past on her bike. At the next cub meeting she asked me how the windows came to be broken.

"It was a bomb, miss," I said desperately. "A small German bomb. Right in the garden."

There had been a smattering of air raids that week, so I thought this was plausible. Baden-Powell and his cubs' promises about truthfulness were, for me, temporarily suspended as an emergency measure. The cub mistress, an earnest, glassy young woman with the strange name of Miss Rabbitt, goggled behind her lenses.

"Oh dear," she said. "Your poor mother! We must all go around and see if we can help her."

"No," I cried. "Mum's in hospital. The bomb blew her arms off."

My old man was stoking boilers in ships' stomachs for most of his life, journeying the world, again and again, searching for whatever sailors search for. He had a funny, agile face with a habit of looking around corners with his mouth and his eyes. His sins were whist drives and whisky.

We hardly ever saw him, but what time he was at home my mother decided was too much. He had a weakness for getting drunk and giving his money away. Sometimes, for variety, he would take up a lost cause in a dockside pub and challenge someone twice his size to a fight. He frequently arrived home plastered (in both senses) and bandaged from his waist to his spreading ears.

On the other hand, I think he loved us dearly in his way. When he sauntered home from his far wanderings he would bring strange toys for us, Roy and myself, and gentle, fragile china, as light as paper, for my mother. This was before their legal separation. My mother would accept with reserved gratefulness the Japanese coffee set, or the tea set from Macao, wash it tenderly and set it proudly with her collection on the Welsh dresser.

Then three nights later the old man would spoil himself, come home raving from the Dock Hotel, and be turfed out once more. When a bomb demolished the Dock Hotel he took us all down to see the ruins. There we were, mother impatient to get home and probably feeling that Hitler had at last achieved something good; Roy and I, in our raincoats, wondering that so many bricks could have gone to make one building; and dad, his eyes groping over the debris in eloquent sorrow. Other men were standing along the pavement in the same stunned, homeless way.

The old man had been a sailor almost from the time he left school, with a break during the first war when he was a soldier. His two elder sons had gone to sea in their teens and had risen, by study and endeavour, to the bridge, while dad doggedly shovelled on in the boiler room. He spent half his life in that steaming hell and I have heard it said that nothing was too heavy or too hot for him. My only prayer for him has been that he was not down there when the torpedo hit his ship.

In his young days he brought despair to his father, a moustached Welsh Baptist and a liberal too, and to his gentle mother, by disappearing for months or even years. Then one deep night they would answer the door and he would be there arrayed in a gaucho's outfit he had won in a poker game in South America.

Once he jumped a ship in Australia and adventured for the goldfields to strike his fortune. Six months later he was in a seaman's hostel in Sydney, broke as a beggar, and a sea captain said he wanted a sailor for a voyage back to England. Jim Thomas willingly put his name on the line and the next morning found the ship.

"Jesu," he used to say when he was telling the story, "there she lay and I couldn't believe what I saw. There's me been a stoker ever since I could lift a shovel of coal and this thing was all masts and rigging like a spider's web."

The schooner took six months of horror and hurricane to get home. My old man, hanging tightly somewhere high in the rigging, reckoned he wept most of the way.

Looking back over the valley of these years it is a strange realisation to me that I seem to know so much more about my father than my mother. Yet it was she who was with us all the time.

She was a small woman, pretty even in her late forties. She was fond of quoting, sentimentally, miracles like the Angels of Mons, or how the singing of "Eternal Father" brought succour to the crying crew of a wrecked steamer off the Glamorgan rocks, as proof that there was a God. But in my memory I can never recall her entering a church.

Her unreliable husband, and the fact that her two eldest sons frequently vanished to distant seas for years and never bothered to write or send money, had led her to expect nothing from them.

This was all she normally received. Her life was a tired serial of house-cleaning jobs, with a spell as a school cleaner and another as a factory sweeper thrown in for variety. One thing was constant; there was never any money to spare.

The first and last time I can remember my parents embracing was in 1938. The year I recall exactly not because the fact that they kissed was such a significant event, unusual though it was, but because of the reason for the kiss.

In Spain the civil war was rolling. My father and my elder brother were involved (on opposite sides, I believe) but strictly in the cause of cash. They were on gun-running ships. The old man's vessel was in Barcelona harbour when an adventurous dive bomber appeared over the housetops and dropped a high explosive bomb right down the funnel.

Coldly the announcer on the BBC news said that all the crew were dead. It was a Newport ship and the curtains were drawn in many streets. My mother did not cry but she hardly said anything all the day. Then from the remote BBC came further news. Some of the men had been picked up. The announcer read the names and my father's was the last one on the list.

He came home, all bandaged up as usual but at least honourably this time. My mother and he crushed together and he let out a yell because she pressed on one of his fractured ribs.

A MOMENT OF RESPECT

Two things I remember about my grandfather:
his threadbare trousers, and the way he adjusted
his half-hunter watch two minutes every day.

When I asked him why he needed to know the time so
exactly, he said a business man could lose a fortune
by being two minutes late for an appointment.

When he died he left two meerschaum pipes
and a gold sovereign on a chain. Somebody
threw the meerschaum pipes away, and

there was argument about the sovereign.
On the day of his burial the church clock chimed
as he was lowered down into the clay, and all
the family advanced their watches by two minutes.

                                        Edwin Brock

1 Why do you think the writer of the prose extract says, "… it is a strange realisation to me that I seem to know so much more about my father than my mother"?

2 What is the attitude of the writer to his family generally?

3 What do you think was the attitude of the family to the grandfather in the poem?

4 There is humour in both the prose extract and in the poem. Chose three examples of this humour and explain how they help us to understand and appreciate the characters.

5 Think of the members of your family. The majority of us would say that we come from very ordinary families but there are inevitably moments which are out of the ordinary or humorous.

    EITHER Imitate the style of the prose extract and write a short part of your own autobiography.

    OR   Write a poem about one of your family.

1) It is odd because you would expect the writer to have more knowledge of his mother as he saw very little of his father in comparrison.

I believe that the writer saw the fact that his father was away from his as a reason to believe they were distant. This is however ironic as it is really the person he was nearest to that he was most apart from.

The writer uses this subtle irony to convey a key element of war, the fact that the further apart he was from someone the greater his emotions, feelings and regard was.

The extract tells of how a part of society during war is forgotten. The people who "stay at home" were not given high regard by their younger generations who would idolise solidars etc.

The passage also shows the reflective mood of the writer who wanted to recollect about all the most memorable and distinct parts of his childhood. These events include the smashed windows, the news broadcast and his parent's kiss in 1938.

2) The writer was ashamed of his family and their situation. This is easily justifiable through the way that he was able to think up such extrodinary excuses for what had happend to the windows.

There is also the fact that the writer refferal to the German bomb as being small. This shows a reluctance to draw attention to the plight of his family at the hands of his father.

There is also an obvious affection for his family members, this is clear through the use of friendly terminclagy such as "my old man." It is a friendly phrase showing deep-rooted affection.

Letts
Q&A

33

ANSWER

3) The grandfather was both loved and respected by his family. Their love for him as their grandfather is illustrated through the way that "there was an argument about the sovereign." This proves that everybody wanted something to remember him by, and as the sovereign was the only item left (after the meerschaum pipes were thrown away), all the relatives wanted it.

The respect that the family had for the old man is expressed in the final stanza when "all the family advanced their watches by two minutes." This was a very respectful act to honour the memory of their grandfather.

4) The humour of the mothers arms being blown off by the bomb gives the reader an insight into the feelings of the writer enabling us to appreciate his predicament.

He was embarrassed about what had happened to his home and family and this audaciously funny fabrication of the truth helps to portray this.

I also believe that it helps us understand the feelings for his mother, he was trying to protect her from public scrutiny. It shows to what lengths he will go to to protect his family.

When the writer tells of his father coming home "plastered" in the comic sense it allows us an insight into the view of the writer. He was obviously aware of the situation and was able to distinguish what was happening, this showed a deal of intelligence for a young person.

Finally the kiss by his parents shows humorous irony. It showed the parents' attitude to each other in an ironic way. This can be interpreted by the way that even in their most tender and loving moment pain was inflicted - through the broken ribs. This indicated that the parents could no longer love each other because there was too much pain involved.

5)   Regimental Routine

His shoes, bag and coat by the door,
The regimental photo on the wall,
The carriage clock strikes 7 o'clock,
He rises and begins the process that started earlier.

Beginning the night before,
Polishing, brushing, measuring, checking, filling.
"Old traditions die hard" he claims,
But modern methods are beyond diskin.

Shiney shoes and a perfect suit,
A board for a back and eyes of steel,
Spotless buttons really gleam,
Thats the regimental routine.

'I didn't mean any harm,' the old man said fumblingly. 'I just wanted to get the best for Benjy.' He was getting teary. 'Don't turn me down, please, Mr Wedge.'

45   Vernon knew a lost cause when he saw one; perhaps he had known from the start how this interview would end. His voice softened.

'I didn't say your boy is guilty, Mr Blesker. All I say is that he's got a bad case. A very bad case.'

Motionless, the old man waited.

50   'All right,' Vernon sighed. 'I'll think it over.'

The police blotter had Benjy Blesker's age down as seventeen. He looked younger. The frightened eyes gave him a look of youthful bewilderment. Vernon wasn't taken in by it; he had seen too many innocent, baby-faced, icy-hearted killers.

The boy's cell was clean, and Benjy himself bore no marks of ill-treatment. He sat
55   on the edge of the bunk and kneaded his hands. When Vernon walked in, he asked him for a cigarette.

Vernon hesitated, then shrugged and offered the pack. 'Why not?' he said. 'If you're old enough to be here.'

Benjy lit up and dropped a tough mask over his boyish features.

60   'You the lawyer my old man hired?'

'That's right. My name is Vernon Wedge.'

'When do I get out of here?'

'You don't, not until the trial. They've refused bail.'

'When's the trial?'

65   'Don't rush it,' Vernon growled. 'We need every minute of delay we can get. Don't think this is going to be easy.'

Benjy leaned back, casual. 'I didn't cut that guy,' he said evenly. 'I didn't have anything to do with it.'

Vernon grunted, and pulled a sheet of handwritten notes out of his pocket.

70   'You admitted that you knew Kenny Tarcher?'

'Sure I knew him. We went to Manual Trades together.'

'They tell me Kenny was a member of a gang called The Aces. You ever run with them?'

'With that bunch?' Benjy sneered, and blew a column of smoke. 'I was a Baron.
75   The Barons don't mix with those bums. You know who they take into that gang? A whole lot of –'

'Never mind,' Vernon snapped. 'We can talk about your social life later. You were a Baron and Kenny was an Ace, so that made you natural enemies. You had a rumble last month, and this Kenny Tarcher beat up on you pretty good. Don't give
80   me any arguments about this, it's ancient history.'

Benjy's mouth was quivering. 'Look, Mr Wedge, we don't have that kind of gang. You know Mr Knapp –'

'The youth worker? I just came from him.'

'He'll tell you about the Barons, Mr Wedge, we're not a bunch of hoods. We got a
85   basketball team and everything.'

Vernon smothered a smile. 'Why do you carry a knife, Benjy?'

'It's no switchblade, Mr Wedge. It's more like a boy scout knife; I mean, they sell 'em all over. I use it for whittlin' and stuff like that.'

'Whittling?' It was hard to hide the sneer. The end of Benjy's cigarette flared, as
90 did his temper.

'Look, whose side are you on? I didn't stick Kenny, somebody else did! I swear I didn't kill him!'

'Take it easy. I'm not making accusations, kid, that's the court's job. Now sit back and relax. I'm going over the story, from the police side, and then you can tell me
95 where they're wrong. Every little thing, understand?'

Benjy swallowed hard. Then he nodded.

'It was ten minutes to midnight on June 21,' Vernon said, watching him. 'You and two other guys were walking down Thurmond Street; you came out of a movie house. Kenny Tarcher came out of the corner apartment building on Thurmond
100 and Avenue C. You bumped into each other, and there was some horseplay. The next thing that happens, you and your pals start running down the street. Kenny falls down and tries to crawl to the stoop of his house. There were two people on the steps. They saw you running. They saw Kenny die, right in front of them. He had an eight-inch gash in his stomach.'

105 Benjy looked sick.

'Ten minutes later, the cops caught up with you in your old man's fuel supply store on Chester Street. The knife was still in your pocket.' He paused.

'I didn't cut him,' the boy said grimly. 'All the rest of that stuff, that's true. But I don't know who cut Kenny.'

110 'Who were the other two guys with you?'

'I never saw 'em before. I met 'em in the movies.'

'Don't give me that!'

'What the hell do you want from me?' Benjy bellowed. 'I tell you I don't know those guys! One of them must have done it, I didn't! When I saw he was hurt, I
115 ran. That's all it was!'

'You had the knife –'

'I didn't use it!'

'That knife is Exhibit A,' the lawyer said. 'You know that, don't you? The witnesses saw you holding it –'

120 'Leave me alone! You ain't here to help me!'

Vernon got up.

'I am, Benjy. The only way you can be helped, kid. I want you to cop a plea.'

'What?'

'I want you to plead guilty. Believe me, it's the only sensible thing to do. You put
125 this case to a jury, I swear you'll be spending the rest of your life in a cage. Plead guilty, and the worst you'll get is twenty years. That's not as bad as it sounds; you'll be eligible for parole in five.'

'I won't do it!' Benjy screamed. 'I'm innocent! I'm not goin' to jail for something I didn't do!'

130 'I'm talking sense, kid, why won't you listen?'

'I didn't do it! I didn't!'

Vernon sighed. The corners of his mouth softened, and he dropped a hand on the boy's shoulder.

'Listen,' he said gently. 'I really want to help you, son.'

135　For a moment, Benjy was still. Then he threw off the arm of sympathy, and snarled at the attorney.

'I'm not your son! I got a father!'

Like father, like son, Vernon thought wryly, looking at the mulish mouth and marble eyes of the old man. He was sure Blesker had a softer side. Under other

140　circumstances, he would smile and tell jokes and hum old-country tunes. Now, faced with the lawyer's blunt advice, he was hard as a rock.

'You've got to talk some sense into him,' Vernon said. 'He doesn't know what's good for him. If he pleads guilty to murder in the second degree, the judge will be lenient.'

145　'But he goes to prison? For something he didn't do?'

'You're his father, Mr Blesker. You're ignoring facts.'

'The facts are wrong!' Blesker put his fists on his knees and pounded them once. When he looked up again, there was a new mood in his eyes. 'You tell me something, Mr Wedge –'

150　'Yes?'

'You don't like to lose cases, am I right? That's what they say about you.'

'Is that bad?'

'If my boy pleads guilty, you don't lose nothing. You still got your good record, right?'

'Do you think that's my only reason?'

155　Blesker shrugged. 'I'm only asking, Mr Wedge. I don't know nothing about the law.'

Unable to refute this accurate estimate of his inner thoughts, Vernon tried to summon up an angry denial and failed. He shrugged his shoulders.

'All right,' he said grudgingly. 'So we plead Not Guilty. I'll do everything I can to make it stick.'

160　Blesker examined his face for signs of sincerity. He seemed satisfied.

Vernon came to the courtroom on opening day with a heart as heavy as his briefcase. Surprisingly, the first day didn't go badly. Judge Angus Dwight had been assigned to the bench. In spite of his dour look, Vernon knew him to be scrupulously fair and sneakily sentimental. Wickers, the prosecuting attorney, was

165　a golden-haired Adonis with a theatrical delivery, a keen mind, and an appeal for the ladies. Fortunately, the empanelled jurors were men with only two exceptions, and they were women far past the age of coquetry. During the first hour, Wickers' facetiousness in his opening remarks drew a rebuke from the judge concerning the seriousness of the affair; Vernon's hopes lifted a notch.

170　But it was his only good day. On the second afternoon, Wickers called a man named Sol Dankers to the witness chair.

'Mr Dankers,' he said smoothly, 'you were present at the time of Kenneth Tarcher's slaying, isn't that so?'

'That's right,' Dankers said heavily. He was a hard-breathing, bespectacled man

175　with a red-veined nose. 'I was sittin' on the stoop, when those kids start foolin' around. Next thing I know, one of 'em's stumbling to the stoop, bleedin' like a pig. He drops dead right at the feet of me and my Mrs. I was an hour gettin' the bloodstains off my shoes.'

'Is that all you saw?'

180 'No, sir. I seen that boy, the one over there, runnin' away with a knife in his hand.'

Then it was Vernon's turn.

'Mr Dankers, is it true your eyesight is impaired?'

'True enough. I'm sixty-two, son, wait 'til you're my age.'

He drew a laugh and a rap of the gavel.

185 'It was almost midnight on a street not particularly well lit. Yet you saw a knife –' he pointed to the table where Exhibit A rested – 'that knife, in Benjamin Blesker's hand?'

'It was sort of flashin' in the light, if you know what I mean. But to tell you the truth, I wouldn't have noticed if Mrs Danker hadn't said, "look at that boy, he's got
190 a knife!"'

The crowd buzzed, and Vernon frowned at the inadvertent hearsay testimony. The damage was done; he didn't even bother to voice a complaint.

Mrs Danker testified next; there was nothing wrong with *her* eyes, she said stoutly, and she knew a knife when she saw one. It was the third witness who did
195 the most harm. He was Marty Knapp, a dedicated youth worker serving the neighbourhood.

'No, Benjy isn't a bad kid,' he said thoughtfully. 'But he had a temper. And he never forgave Kenny Tarcher for the beating he gave him.'

'Then in your opinion,' Wickers said triumphantly, 'this *might* have been a grudge
200 killing? Not just a sudden scuffle or unplanned assault, but a deliberate, cold-blooded –'

Vernon was on his feet, shouting objections. Judge Dwight took his side at once, but the impression was indelible in the collective mind of the jury. When Vernon sat down again, he felt as forlorn as Benjy Blesker looked.

205 On the eve of the fourth day, he went to see him.

'What do you say, Benjy?' he said quietly. 'You see the way things are going? I'm pulling out the whole bag of tricks, and I'm not fooling anybody.'

'Try harder!' Benjy snapped.

'If I knew how to work miracles, I'd work one. Look, this State doesn't like to
210 hang kids, but it's happened before –'

'Hang?' the boy said incredulously. 'You're crazy!'

'Even if you got life, know what that means? Even if you got paroled in twenty years, you'll be thirty-seven years old, almost middle-aged, with a record.'

There were tears flooding Benjy's eyes. It was the first sign of a crumpling
215 defence, and the lawyer moved in swiftly.

'Plead guilty,' he said earnestly. 'Plead guilty, Benjy. It's not too late.'

The boy's head snapped up.

'No!' he screamed. 'I didn't do it!'

The fourth day was the worst of all. Vernon railed mercilessly at the prosecution
220 witnesses. He called Dankers a weak-eyed, boozing liar. He forced Mrs Dankers to admit that she hated the neighbourhood kids, and the Barons especially. He got Knapp, the youth worker, to recite every detail of Benjy's good record. But through it all, the jury shifted restlessly, bored, irritated, obviously unimpressed by the 'character' testimony, eager only for facts, the bloodier the better.

225 Wickers gave them what they wanted. Wickers treated them to a blow-by-blow

re-enactment of the stabbing. He bled for them. He clutched his stomach. He put the victim's mother on the stand. He let her cry through ten minutes of pointless testimony, until even Judge Dwight got sick of the spectacle. But it was working. Vernon, jury-smart, knew it was working.

230 The trial was almost over. Wickers, waving the knife under Benjy Blesker's nose, got him to admit that it was his, admit that he was never without it, admit that he had it in his pocket – maybe even in his hand – the night of the slaying. It was his curtain-closer. Wickers sat down, the prosecution's case stated.

One more day, and it would be finished.

235 There was a weekend hiatus before the trial resumed. Vernon Wedge spent the time thinking.

It was the old man's fault, he thought bitterly. It was the old man Blesker who was behind all the trouble. His faith in Benjy was the indomitable, obstinate faith of the fanatic. Even if the boy was guilty, concern for his father would prevent him
240 from admitting the truth.

'The funny thing is,' he told Olga, his secretary, 'if I was on that jury, I wouldn't know how to vote.'

Olga clucked.

'You don't look well,' she said. 'You look anaemic. When this is over, you ought to
245 see a doctor.'

'A headshrinker, that's what I ought to see.'

'I mean a doctor,' Olga said firmly.

It was then that the idea was born. Vernon looked at his secretary queerly, and stood up behind his desk.

250 'You know, it's a thought. Maybe I ought to see one. You remember Doc Hagerty?'

'No.'

'Sure you remember! On the Hofstraw case, 1958 –'

'But *he's* not the kind of doctor I mean. I mean a good all-around GP.'

'I'm going out,' Vernon said suddenly. 'I'll be at the Dugan Hospital if you need
255 me. But don't bother me unless it's urgent.'

He found Hagerty in the basement laboratory of the Dugan Hospital. Olga was right: Hagerty was no chest-thumping, tongue-depressing practitioner; he was more biochemist than physician. But he was what Vernon needed.

Hagerty was a white-haired man with shoulders rounded from years of bending
260 over microscopes, and he smelled vaguely of sulphur. He turned out to be ignorant of the trial. Vernon summarised the facts briefly, and then talked about blood.

'You mean there were no benzidine tests made?' Hagerty said quickly. 'Of the murder weapon?'

'Yes,' Vernon admitted, 'and the test proved negative. There weren't any
265 bloodstains on the knife, you understand, it was clean. The prosecution claims that all traces were wiped or washed off. It's never been much of an issue up till now. But I once heard you talk about a more sensitive test than benzidine –'

'There is,' Hagerty grunted. 'Benzidine is the standard blood test in this city, but there's another one. It's a lot more delicate, in my opinion, and it's not always
270 employed. It's called the reduced phenolphthalein test, and depending on a couple of factors, it might be just what you're looking for.'

'What factors?'

'The quality of the blade metal, for one thing. And even if the metal is porous enough to retain microscopic particles of blood, it may be impossible to determine
275 *whose*. If your boy ever cut his finger, or somebody else –'

'What do we have to do?' Vernon said excitedly.

'Get me the knife.'

'That's impossible. It's court property at the moment.'

'Then get me a half a dozen like it.'

280 The lawyer spent all of Saturday morning searching for the weapon's counterpart. His mental picture of it was sharp; he even remembered the letters at the base of the blade: B.L. CO. USA.

He finally found one in a dingy variety store four blocks from the scene of the stabbing. The proprietor had exactly five left in stock; he took them all.

285 There was a two-hour wait that afternoon before he could see Hagerty again; when the white-haired doctor joined him in the laboratory, he didn't apologise.

'I have the solution all ready,' he said crisply. 'You sure this is the same make of knife?'

'Positive.'

Hagerty sprung the large blade. Then he removed a bottle of whole blood from a
290 cabinet, and dipped it inside. Vernon swallowed in revulsion as Hagerty wiped the blade clean with a soft cloth, and marked the knife with a pencil.

'Any trace?' he said, offering it for examination.

'Clean as a whistle.'

Hagerty brought all five blades to a beaker filled with a murky liquid. Vernon
295 helped him open all the knives, and they were ready for the demonstration.

'Mix 'em up good,' Hagerty said. 'It's like a magic trick; you shuffle 'em up, I'll find the one.'

Vernon scrambled the knives. Then, one by one, Hagerty dipped them into the solution.

300 The third one turned the liquid pink. It was the knife that had been marked.

'It works,' Vernon breathed. 'It really works.'

'The metal is porous. If there were bloodstains on it from years ago, this test would show it up.'

'Thank you,' Vernon said humbly. 'You've saved my life, Doc.'

305 '*Your* life?' Hagerty said dryly.

When Vernon entered Benjy's cell, the boy was reading a pulp magazine with intense concentration. He seemed detached, disinterested. Vernon understood it; he had seen this before in the condemned.

'Listen to me,' he said harshly. 'Listen good. I have an idea that might save you,
310 but I have to know the truth.'

'I told you everything –'

'There's a test,' the lawyer said. 'A test that can determine whether or not there was ever blood on that knife of yours.'

'So?'

315 'I propose to make that test in court on Monday. If it's negative, the jury will know you didn't kill Kenny Tarcher.'

'I don't understand that kind of stuff –'

'I'm not asking you to understand,' Vernon said tautly. 'If you stabbed that boy, a solution is going to turn pink and you can kiss your freedom goodbye. What's more, if you ever cut *anybody* with that knife, even yourself, it'll turn pink. So I want you to tell me now. *Was there ever blood on that knife?*'

'I told you I didn't cut him!'

'You moron!' Vernon shouted. 'Do you understand my question? Was there ever blood of *any* kind on that knife?'

'No! It was brand-new. I never cut anybody with it.'

'You're sure? Absolutely sure?'

'I told you, didn't I?'

'This is scientific stuff, boy, don't think you can fool a test tube!'

'I said it's clean!'

Vernon Wedge sighed, and stood up.

'Okay, Benjy. We'll see how clean it is. We'll give it a bath. And God help you if you lied to me.'

On Monday, Wickers rose to make his final peroration. He was bland-faced, a picture of confidence. Vernon looked at the vacant faces of the jurors, waiting for their emotional rubdown. But he wasn't going to allow it.

He stood up, and addressed Judge Dwight.

'Your Honour, something occurred over the weekend which I consider of paramount importance to this case. I ask the court's permission to introduce new evidence.'

'Objection,' Wickers said calmly. 'The defence has had sufficient time for the introduction of evidence. I suggest this is a delaying tactic.'

Vernon looked defeated, but he was only playing possum. Judge Dwight prompted him.

'What sort of evidence, Mr Wedge?'

'It's a demonstration, Your Honour,' he said weakly. 'In my opinion, it will clearly establish my client's guilt or innocence. But if the court rules –'

'Very well, Mr Wedge, you may proceed.'

Quickly, Vernon undid the clasps of the black box in front of him. He removed the wide-mouthed beaker, and then the foil lid that covered it. He brought the murky solution to the bench that held the trial exhibits.

'And what is this?' Judge Dwight said.

'This, Your Honour, is a chemical solution formulated for the detection of blood.'

The courtroom buzzed; on the prosecution's side of the room, there was a hurried consultation.

Vernon faced the jurors.

'Ladies and gentlemen, Exhibit A in this case is the knife which presumably killed Kenneth Tarcher. This is the knife which was in the possession of Benjamin Blesker the night of the slaying. Yet not one shred of testimony has been heard during this trial concerning the vital factor of *blood.*'

He picked up the knife, and sprung the long, shining blade.

'This knife!' he said, waving it in the air. 'Look at it carefully. It has never left the court's possession since my client's arrest. Yet this clean, shiny blade can still tell a story of guilt or innocence. For as every biochemist knows, there is an infallible test which can determine whether an object of such porous metal has *ever* been stained with even one drop of *blood*!'

He poised the knife over the mouth of the beaker.

'Ladies and gentlemen, I intend to prove once and for all whether I have been defending a boy falsely accused, or a lying murderer. I intend to dip this blade in the solution. If it turns pink – you must punish him for his guilt. If it remains clear – you must do what is just, and set him free.'

Slowly, he brought the knife down.

'Your Honour!'

Wickers was on his feet, and Vernon halted.

'Your Honour, objection! Objection!'

'Yes, Mr Wickers?'

Wickers' eyes flashed angrily. 'Defence counsel is acting improperly. The police laboratory has already made the standard benzidine test of the weapon and found no bloodstains on the blade. We admit that the knife has been cleansed –'

'Your Honour,' Vernon said loudly, 'the sensitivity of this test far exceeds the benzidine –'

'This performance is irrelevant, immaterial, and completely improper!' Wickers whirled to the jury. 'At no time during this trial has the prosecution denied the absence of blood on Benjamin Blesker's knife. Any so-called "test" that corroborates this is completely gratuitous, and is intended as pure theatrics to mislead and befuddle the jury! I demand this farcical demonstration be stopped!'

There was a moment's silence. Vernon looked up at the judge hopefully, waiting.

Dwight folded his hands.

'Mr Wedge, I'm afraid you're not in a position to qualify as an expert in forensic chemistry. And, as Mr Wickers says, mere corroboration of the police laboratory report is gratuitous evidence that cannot be properly admitted. Therefore, the objection is sustained.'

'But Your Honour –'

'Sustained,' Judge Dwight said gravely. 'You cannot make the test, Mr Wedge.'

His summation was the briefest of his career.

'I believe Benjamin Blesker is innocent,' he said wearily. 'I believe this because of a test I was not permitted to make. This boy knew that the results of this test might have condemned him, yet he told me to proceed. No guilty man would have allowed it; no innocent man would have had it any other way.'

The jury was out less than an hour. When they returned, they declared that Benjamin Blesker was innocent.

Vernon was permitted the use of an adjoining chamber for a meeting with his client. It wasn't a victory celebration. The boy seemed stunned, and the happiness in old man Blesker's face looked more like sorrow. When the lawyer entered the room, he stood up shakily and held out his hand.

'God bless you,' he whispered. 'Bless you for what you did.'

'I didn't come to be congratulated,' Vernon said coldly. 'I wanted to see you both for another reason.'

The bailiff entered, and placed the beaker on the desk. When he left, Vernon took
the knife out of his pocket, and put it down beside the beaker. The old man picked
410   it up and looked at the weapon as if he had never seen it before.

'Wickers was right,' Vernon said flatly. 'What I did out there was theatrics. I didn't
want to make the demonstration; I was counting on the prosecution halting it.'

'You didn't want to?' Blesker said blankly. 'You didn't want to make the test?'

'I could have gotten an expert, a real one, like Doc Hagerty. But I didn't want to
415   take the chance; if this stuff turned red ...' He looked at the beaker and frowned.
'No,' he said. 'The risk was too great. If Wickers had played along, I would have
been forced to do it. But I figured they would object, and the jury would be
impressed the right way. They were, thank God.'

Blesker let out a long sigh.

420   'But now there's something we have to do,' Vernon said. 'Something to satisfy
us all.'

'What do you mean?'

Vernon looked at the boy. Benjy wouldn't meet his eyes.

'I still don't know the truth,' the lawyer said. 'I don't know it, and neither do you.
425   Only Benjy here knows it.'

'You can't mean that! You said yourself –'

'Never mind what I said out there. There's only one way we can really know,
Mr Blesker.'

He held out his hand.

430   'Give me the knife, Mr Blesker. We're going to make the test the judge wouldn't
allow. For our own sakes.'

'But why?' the old man cried. 'What difference does it make?'

'*Because I want to know!* Even if you don't, Mr Blesker, I want to know!'

'Give me the knife,' Vernon said.

435   Blesker picked up the knife. He touched its cool blade thoughtfully.

'Of course,' he said.

Then, slowly, he drew the blade deliberately across the back of his hand. The
sharp edge bit deep. Blood welled like a crimson river in the cut and stained his
hand, his cuff, his sleeve, the surface of the desk. He looked at the wound sadly,
440   indifferently, and then handed the dripping weapon to the attorney.

'Make your test,' he said dreamily. 'Make your test now, Mr Wedge.'

And as Vernon stared at him, he removed a crumpled handkerchief from his
pocket and wound it around his injured hand. Then he took his son's arm, and
they left the room together.

Kiss Miss Carol by Farrukh Dhondy

Jolil knew that his Dad would not be at home when he got back from school. Mr Miah would come home at seven o'clock, sometimes eight, after he finished work at the tailoring factory. When he got back he'd say his sunset prayers, even though in England the sun had gone to rest hours earlier, and then he'd seat Jolil
5 on the stool next to him and ask him what had happened at school. He'd look through Jolil's school satchel and flip the pages of the books one by one. Jolil knew his father didn't read English very well, but day after day, especially since he'd gone to the new school, the pretence was kept up. Today Jolil carried Miss Ingram's letter in his bag. He didn't want to give it to his Dad. On the
10 envelope, Miss Ingram had written 'Mr and Mrs Miah'. When his Dad saw the letter he would think it was a complaint. He'd hold the letter up to the light and then ask Jolil to read it.

'Podho, podho,' he'd say in Bengali, 'Read loudly your own sins.' The letter wasn't a complaint. It was an invitation from the school to the Christmas Concert.
15 'You can read them, but then put them away and make sure your parents leave the evening free,' Miss Ingram said.

When Jolil went to her desk as his name was called, she smiled and said: 'Won't his mother be proud of her Jolil when she sees him speaking such good English? Have you asked her to patch a shirt for you yet?'

20 'Yes Miss, I'll bring it tomorrow,' Jolil said. It wasn't the truth. He hadn't mentioned the shirt at home. In fact he hadn't mentioned the Christmas play at all since the day he first told his Dad about it.

Miss Ingram had read the play in the English lesson and then they'd read different parts in class. It was called *A Christmas Carol*. Then when they'd
25 finished reading it, they had to read the parts one by one in front of Miss Ingram and the Headmaster. Miss Ingram had said that only those girls and boys who read loudly and clearly would be given the parts to act on stage. Jolil was one of the best readers in the class and the others had only laughed at him once when he said 'kiss-miss' and the Headmaster stopped him and said, 'No, don't kiss miss
30 now, wait for Kris-t-mas'.

At the end of it, Miss Ingram read out the list. 'And we've decided that Jolil must be Tiny Tim,' she beamed. It was only when he was going home that day that Jolil wondered what his Dad would say. He wouldn't like it. More waste of time, he'd say.

35 'What part are you supposed to be playing?' his Dad asked. 'Plays all the time, no good.'

'It's Tiny Tim,' Jolil said.

'What's that?'

'It's a boy, a lame boy.'

40 'Any other Bengali children in this play?'

'The whole class. There's Mumtaz and Mahashobha.'

'I suppose they are lame too?'

'No Dad, it's a very good story, about Christmas; about being kind to the poor.'

'What are you acting? Kind or poor?'

45   'Poor,' Jolil replied. It wasn't going well, this questioning.

'I send you to school clean and they turn you into a beggar boy!' his Dad said.

Then he took off his white cap and scratched his almost bald head. 'You tell them Allah gave you both legs to use. Playing beggars, very bad.'

That was a month ago and so Jolil didn't tell his Dad about the rehearsals and
50   how much he enjoyed himself hopping about on the crutch and being helped to his stool by Paul and Rebecca who were acting as his brother and sister Cratchits. There was another reason Jolil didn't want to show his Dad the invitation. Even if by some miracle he changed his mind and said yes, he could be in the play and go to school in the evening when the parents would come, Jolil didn't want his Dad
55   to come to his school. The last time he came, he turned up in his prayer-cap, wearing his loose white trousers and long black coat. The other boys and girls didn't have Dads like that. All their Dads wore flash jackets and even Mumtaz's Dad was young and wore a suit, and when he saw Jolil said, 'Hullo sonny'.

Jolil wasn't really ashamed of his Dad, but school was a different world and he
60   felt shy going around with him and sitting at the teachers' tables and listening to his Dad's broken English.

Now he had this invitation. He walked out of the school gate and decided to walk all the way home and not towards the bus stop. He walked past the corrugated iron fences around the old estates which were being gutted and rebuilt or
65   demolished completely. With their windows and frames ripped out, they looked like huge skulls which had been picked clean, Jolil thought.

Jolil reached Liverpool Street. He crossed carefully. There was lots of traffic, and thousands of white people hurrying towards the train station. Nothing to fear from them Jolil thought, they were the kind of white people who didn't bother
70   you, his Dad had told him. His brother Khalil had said that when white people have something to do then they don't notice you. It was true. Once across Liverpool Street, Jolil knew he had to watch out. Beyond that boundary there was the vegetable market and then the alleys and streets with the big old estates. Very few Bengalis lived in those estates. Once when he was walking home from school,
75   some young white men on a balcony had watched him and shouted bad things at him and one of them threw a bucket of soapy water from the first floor all over him. Jolil got home soaking and told his mother it had been raining the other side of Brick Lane. She wouldn't know. She hardly went out, ever.

After Brick Lane it was safe. Nearly everybody on Brick Lane and the streets
80   beyond it was Bengali or Punjabi or Indian or something. If anyone stopped him in the street it would probably be someone who recognised him as his father's son and was from his father's village back in Bangladesh.

Walking down Hanbury Street, only two hundred yards from where he lived, Jolil made up his mind. The invitation would have to go. He'd tear it up. Then on the
85   day of the concert, he'd tell his Dad that he was going to the pictures with his elder brother Khalil who was allowed out of the house at any time, now that he was sixteen.

If he saved up all the bus fares his mother gave him and walked to and from school every day and gave up eating crisps, then he could save enough to bribe
90   Khalil with it by buying him a ticket to the Naz Cinema on the day and ask him to wait for him after the movie and go home with him.

He pulled the envelope out of his bag and looked at it hard, then he tore it down the middle. Then again and again until the wad of paper was too thick to tear. He threw the pieces near a pile of garbage and the lines of the play came into his
95   head 'God bless us, one and all.'

Now he'd done it. He looked around. He suddenly felt lighter, like a donkey who'd thrown off its rider. It would be all right, he told himself, Khalil would agree. Then he could buy himself a second-hand shirt from Dog Market and he could sew up one sleeve and put patches on the shirt when his Dad was out of the house. There were two sewing machines at home. His Dad was a tailor, his Mum was a tailor, his brother, even though he was in the Sixth Form, was a bit of a machinist and Jolil could certainly use the machines. He knew about the machines like white boys and girls knew about knives and forks. Jolil reached for his front door key. He thought he heard Khalil's voice. Then he heard his Dad's voice. He went into the front room. Khalil was standing in front of the mirror and combing his hair, pretending not to look at his Dad but observing his face in the mirror.

'You'll do exactly as I say,' their Dad said. Khalil scowled and didn't reply.

'No factory today?' Jolil asked.

'Don't interrupt,' his Dad said, 'go into the kitchen.'

Jolil did as he was told. His mother was sitting on a stool and sorting out the grit and chaff from a tray of lentils. She was also listening to the argument between father and son in the front room. She didn't say a word to Jolil. Khalil was making some reply. He didn't want to go, he said. Jolil gathered the story. His father was telling Khalil that he had to go with his uncle back to Bangladesh for four months. He had to leave in two days' time. His ticket had been bought. There was family business to settle in their village and he was the eldest son and had to go back and see it done.

It was obvious that Khalil didn't want to go to Bangladesh, even for a few months. Both the brothers, Jolil and Khalil, knew all about their village there. Khalil had been born there, but Jolil had been born in Britain and had grown up in the East End. Khalil always talked about Bangladesh as his real country, but now that he had to go, he didn't want to. But if the family said you had to go, then you had to go. It would be bad with Khalil, Jolil thought. Then it struck him that his plan, the big lie, getting out of the house on the evening of the Christmas show, would now be impossible. Maybe God had punished him. He thought about it all through school the next day. Should he tell Miss Ingram? Darren could be given the part. He'd learn the lines and do it. Miss Ingram would ask him to change places with Darren who was only helping move the tables and things onto the stage and hated it. Jolil couldn't even do that. He had to say he wouldn't be there.

Besides, if he told Miss Ingram, she might want to come home and speak to his Dad. That was what she was like. Jolil looked at Miss Ingram. She had curly blonde hair, all untidy and her jeans were patched. He knew his father wouldn't like her. He wouldn't listen to her. Maybe if she wore a neat skirt and a clean shirt and combed her hair, then his Dad would listen to her, but Jolil couldn't ask her to do that. The day Khalil was going to the airport, Miss Ingram told the class that they were going to try some costumes on. 'Up with your leg, Jolil,' she said. 'Let's see if we can make a real hobbler out of you. We're going to tie your left leg behind your back and then put you into these beautiful big bloomers.'

Most of them knew their lines by now and, with the costumes, the play suddenly felt very real. That evening his Dad didn't ask to see his school books. Instead he sat Jolil down and told him that now Khalil had gone, he would have to work much harder and his mother would have to work too, because he had spent a great deal of money on Khalil's trip and they had to make it up.

'You can get back straight from school and help your mother. I've found a guv'nor who will give us pocket linings to sew and I'll bring the bundles home tomorrow. You want to do it, don't you?'

Jolil said yes, he did. His father patted him on the shoulder. He looked worried and his eyes seemed to look beyond the wall he was staring at. 'You're a good boy,' he said.

150 There was only one day left before the play now. Jolil couldn't tell Miss Ingram that he wouldn't be there. Maybe if he spoke really loudly and clearly when the school were watching the play in the afternoon, then she would forgive him when he didn't turn up in the evening. Jolil remembered the time when a small Bengali boy had been kidnapped in the East End. Maybe he could tell the Headmaster the
155 day after the play that he had been kidnapped by some men in masks and they had taken him away. Or he could say he suddenly fainted in the street on the way to school. Jolil woke up on the morning of the play to the sound of the clicking machine. His Dad had been out early that day and returned with the stuff that had to be stitched. In the front room his mother was already at work. Jolil had
160 two hours before school. He made himself some tea, changed into his school clothes and sat down at the other machine. He watched the clock. He watched the needle go in and out of the patches of grey cloth, like the beak of a bird pecking down a line of crumbs. He turned the linings on the steel plate with a flourish, like a driver turning the wheel round a fast corner. His Dad left for work.

165 'I have to go to school, Mum,' Jolil said.

'Do as you please. I'm tied to this machine. What's so important about your school anyway? You can stay home one day. There are two thousand to do.'

'I've already done two hundred.'

'They have to be finished by this evening. Then your father says we'll get another
170 load of coat linings to do. You'll have to go with him this evening and get the bundles.'

Jolil was late for school. By the time he got there, the Maths lesson had already started.

After dinner the actors were called by the loudspeaker system they had in each
175 class to the rooms at the back of the hall. In the hall the seniors were putting out the chairs. The third years had a reggae band on stage and there were wires, baskets of costumes from the fifth year play, overturned chairs and running teachers all over the place. Miss Ingram was helping people on with their costumes and then sending them to a corner of the room where two art teachers
180 sat them down on a stool in front of a bright light and put pink stuff on their faces. It wasn't like school. Even the lights in the room were brighter and stood on stands. It was snowing outside.

Jolil could hear the rest of the school filing in and the teachers seeing that they sat down. The first item was the reggae band. The murmur, like the roar of a railway
185 station, died down in a few seconds after the first note rang out in the hall. It was good. The school loved it. Jolil could hear the claps and his heart began to beat faster. Miss Ingram kept telling those who were whispering to each other to shut up. She had brought Jolil a battered hat with a turned up brim, like Paddington Bear wore, and he had to put it on. Jolil thought he'd be scared when he saw all
190 the faces of the school looking up at him, but when he actually got on stage and the words came tumbling out of him, and he turned his eyes to look into the hall, all he could see was darkness and outlines.

The school clapped wildly when the play was done and the curtains came down and the lights went up. 'Good show, all of you,' the Headmaster said as they were
195 changing back into their own clothes. 'If you do as well this evening, we'll give the whole school a holiday some time next term.'

'What's the matter, Jolil?' asked Miss Ingram. 'You were perfect. Are you feeling all right?'

'Yes Miss,' Jolil replied and immediately realised that he should have said 'No
Miss' and then they might believe him if he said he was ill and couldn't come that
evening. 'I'm the traitor, Miss. No holiday for the school. We won't do as well this
evening. You see, my Dad, he doesn't like plays, he doesn't listen to anybody. He
won't let me come. The linings, Miss, the coat linings, we've got to do the coat
linings. I'm sorry, I'm very, very sorry.' The words were tumbling around Jolil's
mind. 'My Dad is Scrooge,' he wanted to say. 'If you were an angel, a good spirit,
he'd listen to you. No! He wouldn't listen to anybody.'

'Come back at six. The play will start at seven-thirty,' Miss Ingram said.

It was on the way home, after he crossed Brick Lane, that Jolil began to feel that
maybe his Dad was right. All these men and boys in Brick Lane, moving here and
there, some with hangers and coats in their hands, they were all working. His
Dad said Britain was where he'd come to sell his sweat, not to play silly tricks.
Jolil felt he was one of them. He was not like the white children. His family wasn't
like theirs. They didn't have to sit at a machine and do linings at home. They read
comics and played with the other boys and girls on their estates. When he got
home his mother was still at the sewing machine.

'Count those for me, wrap them up in bundles,' she said, throwing a stitched
pocket to the floor on top of a heap. Jolil bundled the cloth up and then sat at the
other machine and started it humming.

By the time his Dad returned it was six-thirty. The linings were all done and his
Mum was cleaning up the front room. 'We've got to take time on them. Learn
about time. Learn to keep to the agreements you make,' his Dad said. Then he
asked him to fetch his canvas bag. They were setting out.

At seven-thirty Miss Ingram would realise that he wasn't coming. They would all
be there in the changing room, their faces painted and ready. Jolil tried to put it
out of his mind as he gripped the bags and belted his coat about him. The roads
were thick with snow and they picked their way carefully through the slush, not
talking to each other and looking down. They stopped outside an old building and
Jolil's Dad rang the bell.

'Ah, about time Miah,' the white man said as he asked them to follow him up the
stairs. 'I've got contracts and deadlines too, you know.'

'You said Thursday, we bring Thursday,' Mr Miah said.

'Yeah, right,' the man said, spreading the linings from the bag onto the table.
There were coats being stitched lying on the machines and on the floor of the
dingy room.

'Now you want the silk set. I'll get it by next Monday, won't I?' the guv'nor asked.

'You say it date, we bring it date,' Mr Miah said.

'That's a good lad,' the man said and took Jolil's Dad to the back room and came
back with piles and piles of green cloth. They stuffed the cloth into the bags and
descended the stairs. They walked down the deserted street and turned right
towards the railway bridge which would bring them out of the dead land. Mr
Miah carried three bags, and Jolil two.

As they walked, a white van drove past them and then stopped a few yards
ahead. As they came up to pass it, a man leaned out of the passenger window and
shouted.

'Oi, Ayatollah, what've you got there? Rat curry?'

'Come this way,' his Dad said. 'These are rubbish people making trouble. Don't
say nothing to him.' He spoke in English because he wanted the men to
understand. The door of the van opened and the man stepped out. Another man

250 jumped out after him. Jolil didn't have time to notice what they looked like. His father jerked him by the arm and turned him around.

'Back to the guv'nor factory,' he said. They were walking fast now. Jolil turned his head and saw the two men jump back in the van which was starting up its engine.

255 'Are they coming?' his Dad asked. The van turned, skidded in the snow, went past them very fast and braked suddenly at the entrance to the alley towards which they were headed.

'We were talking to you, Ayatollah. You're obviously in a hurry.'

'No talking,' his Dad said. He and Jolil were turning round to go back the other way again.

260 'Chewing a brick then?' the second man said. There must be three of them, Jolil thought, one driving and these two ruffians. Again the van started up after them, went past them and blocked the road. The three men jumped out. Again Jolil and his Dad turned round. They were running now and for a hundred yards the men chased them.

265 They reached a street Jolil knew. 'This way,' Jolil said. They turned two corners. There were no footsteps behind them now.

'We've lost them,' his Dad said and just then the headlights of the van turned the corner.

'Come on,' Jolil shouted in Bengali. He looked at his Dad who was panting heavily
270 now. 'My school is just here, there'll be people there,' Jolil said. His feet hardly touched the snow. The van caught up with them and swerved to hit them, missed and then came to a dead stop and started again. His Dad was two feet behind him, another car passed them and drove into the school gate which was a few yards ahead now. By its headlights, Jolil saw a crowd of people gathered at the
275 gate. The white van paused outside the gate, and then Jolil saw it slowly move on. Jolil was in the thick of the crowd, holding his chest, pulling at his breath. There were teachers and some pupils and the caretaker and Miss Ingram.

'Thank God you've come,' she said. 'Hello, Mr Miah. You brought him just in time. Ian will show you where to sit.' She grabbed Jolil and propelled him towards the
280 changing room. 'What happened to you? I thought you'd been kidnapped or something. We've got five minutes to get you changed. They've put the fifth year play on first because of you. Never mind now, just catch your breath.'

'Jolil's here,' the word spread.

Jolil rushed onto the stage, limping and his hat fell off. He heard the polite
285 subdued giggles of the audience. Then he gathered himself. He was going to do it good. After that the play went beautifully.

'God bless us, one and all,' Jolil heard himself say, casting his crutch on the stage as he knelt down as Miss Ingram had taught him to do.

All he could see was the outline of the footlights as the applause deafened him.
290 Somewhere beyond those lights was his Dad, still gathering his breath. Or maybe he had stepped out on the streets again, looking for the bags they'd dropped.

Flight by Doris Lessing

Above the old man's head was the dovecote, a tall wire-netted shelf on stilts, full of strutting, preening birds. The sunlight broke on their grey breasts into small rainbows. His ears were lulled by their crooning, his hands stretched up towards the favourite, a homing pigeon, a young plump-bodied bird which stood still when it saw him and cocked a shrewd bright eye.

'Pretty, pretty, pretty,' he said, as he grasped the bird and drew it down, feeling the cold coral claws tighten around his finger. Content, he rested the bird lightly on his chest, and leaned against a tree, gazing out beyond the dovecote into the landscape of a late afternoon. In folds and hollows of sunlight and shade, the dark red soil, which was broken into great dusty clods, stretched wide to a tall horizon. Trees marked the course of the valley; a stream of rich green grass the road.

His eyes travelled homewards along this road until he saw his granddaughter swinging on the gate underneath a frangipani tree. Her hair fell down her back in a wave of sunlight, and her long bare legs repeated the angles of the frangipani stems, bare, shining-brown stems among patterns of pale blossoms.

She was gazing past the pink flowers, past the railway cottage where they lived, along the road to the village.

His mood shifted. He deliberately held out his wrist for the bird to take flight, and caught it again at the moment it spread its wings. He felt the plump shape strive and strain under his fingers; and, in a sudden access of troubled spite, shut the bird into a small box and fastened the bolt. 'Now you stay there,' he muttered; and turned his back on the shelf of birds. He moved warily along the hedge, stalking his granddaughter, who was now looped over the gate, her head loose on her arms, singing. The light happy sound mingled with the crooning of the birds, and his anger mounted.

'Hey!' he shouted; saw her jump, look back, and abandon the gate. Her eyes veiled themselves, and she said in a pert neutral voice: 'Hullo, Grandad.' Politely she moved towards him, after a lingering backward glance at the road.

'Waiting for Steven, hey?' he said, his fingers curling like claws into his palm.

'Any objection?' she asked lightly, refusing to look at him.

He confronted her, his eyes narrowed, shoulders hunched, tight in a hard knot of pain which included the preening birds, the sunlight, the flowers. He said: 'Think you're old enough to go courting, hey?'

The girl tossed her head at the old-fashioned phrase and sulked, 'Oh, Grandad!'

'Think you want to leave home, hey? Think you can go running around the fields at night?'

Her smile made him see her, as he had every evening of this warm end-of-summer month, swinging hand in hand along the road to the village with that red-handed, red-throated, violent-bodied youth, the son of the postmaster. Misery went to his head and he shouted angrily: 'I'll tell your mother!'

'Tell away!' she said, laughing, and went back to the gate.

He heard her singing, for him to hear:

'I've got you under my skin,

I've got you deep in the heart of ...'

45 'Rubbish,' he shouted. 'Rubbish. Impudent little bit of rubbish!'

Growling under his breath he turned towards the dovecote, which was his refuge from the house he shared with his daughter and her husband and their children. But now the house would be empty. Gone all the young girls with their laughter and their squabbling and their teasing. He would be left, uncherished and alone,
50 with that square-fronted, calm-eyed woman, his daughter.

He stopped, muttering, before the dovecote, resenting the absorbed cooing birds.

From the gate the girl shouted: 'Go and tell! Go on, what are you waiting for?'

Obstinately he made his way to the house, with quick, pathetic persistent glances of appeal back at her. But she never looked around. Her defiant but anxious
55 young body stung him into love and repentance. He stopped, 'But I never meant ...' he muttered, waiting for her to turn and run to him. 'I didn't mean ...'

She did not turn. She had forgotten him. Along the road came the young man Steven, with something in his hand. A present for her? The old man stiffened as he watched the gate swing back, and the couple embrace. In the brittle shadows
60 of the frangipani tree his granddaughter, his darling, lay in the arms of the postmaster's son, and her hair flowed back over his shoulder.

'I see you!' shouted the old man spitefully. They did not move. He stumped into the little whitewashed house, hearing the wooden veranda creak angrily under his feet. His daughter was sewing in the front room, threading a needle held to
65 the light.

He stopped again, looking back into the garden. The couple were now sauntering among the bushes, laughing. As he watched he saw the girl escape from the youth with a sudden mischievous movement, and run off through the flowers with him in pursuit. He heard shouts, laughter, a scream, silence.

70 'But it's not like that at all,' he muttered miserably. 'It's not like that. Why can't you see? Running and giggling, and kissing and kissing. You'll come to something quite different.'

He looked at his daughter with sardonic hatred, hating himself. They were caught and finished, both of them, but the girl was still running free.

75 'Can't you *see*?' he demanded of his invisible granddaughter, who was at that moment lying in the thick green grass with the postmaster's son.

His daughter looked at him and her eyebrows went up in tired forbearance.

'Put your birds to bed?' she asked, humouring him.

'Lucy,' he said urgently, 'Lucy ...'

80 'Well, what is it now?'

'She's in the garden with Steven.'

'Now you just sit down and have your tea.'

He stumped his feet alternately, thump, thump, on the hollow wooden floor and shouted: 'She'll marry him. I'm telling you, she'll be marrying him next!'

85 His daughter rose swiftly, brought him a cup, set him a plate.

'I don't want any tea. I don't want it, I tell you.'

'Now, now,' she crooned. 'What's wrong with it? Why not?'

'She's eighteen. Eighteen!'

'I was married at seventeen and I never regretted it.'

90 'Liar,' he said. 'Liar. Then you should regret it. Why do you make your girls marry? It's you who do it. What do you do it for? Why?'

'The other three have done fine. They've three fine husbands. Why not Alice?'

'She's the last,' he mourned. 'Can't we keep her a bit longer?'

'Come, now, Dad. She'll be down the road, that's all. She'll be here every day to
95 see you.'

'But it's not the same.' He thought of the other three girls, transformed inside a few months from charming petulant spoiled children into serious young matrons.

'You never did like it when we married,' she said. 'Why not? Every time, it's the same. When I got married you made me feel like it was something wrong. And my
100 girls the same. You get them all crying and miserable the way you go on. Leave Alice alone. She's happy.' She sighed, letting her eyes linger on the sunlit garden. 'She'll marry next month. There's no reason to wait.'

'You've said they can marry?' he said incredulously.

'Yes, Dad, why not?' she said coldly, and took up her sewing.

105 His eyes stung, and he went out on to the veranda. Wet spread down over his chin and he took out a handkerchief and mopped his whole face. The garden was empty.

From around the corner came the young couple; but their faces were no longer set against him. On the wrist of the postmaster's son balanced a young pigeon, the
110 light gleaming on its breast.

'For me?' said the old man, letting the drops shake off his chin. 'For me?'

'Do you like it?' The girl grabbed his hand and swung on it. 'It's for you, Grandad. Steven brought it for you.' They hung about him, affectionate, concerned, trying to charm away his wet eyes and his misery. They took his arms and directed him
115 to the shelf of birds, one on each side, enclosing him, petting him, saying wordlessly that nothing would be changed, nothing could change, and that they would be with him always. The bird was proof of it, they said, from their lying happy eyes, as they thrust it on him. 'There, Grandad, it's yours. It's for you.'

They watched him as he held it on his wrist, stroking its soft, sun-warmed back,
120 watching the wings lift and balance.

'You must shut it up for a bit,' said the girl intimately. 'Until it knows this is its home.'

'Teach your grandmother to suck eggs,' growled the old man.

Released by his half-deliberate anger, they fell back, laughing at him. 'We're glad you like it.' They moved off, now serious and full of purpose, to the gate, where
125 they hung, backs to him, talking quietly. More than anything could, their grown-up seriousness shut him out, making him alone; also, it quietened him, took the sting out of their tumbling like puppies on the grass. They had forgotten him again. Well, so they should, the old man reassured himself, feeling his throat clotted with tears, his lips trembling. He held the new bird to his face, for the
130 caress of its silken feathers. Then he shut it in a box and took out his favourite.

'*Now* you can go,' he said aloud. He held it poised, ready for flight, while he looked down the garden towards the boy and the girl. Then, clenched in the pain of loss, he lifted the bird on his wrist, and watched it soar. A whirr and a spatter of wings, and a cloud of birds rose into the evening from the dovecote.

135 At the gate Alice and Steven forgot their talk and watched the birds.

On the veranda, that woman, his daughter, stood gazing, her eyes shaded with a hand that still held her sewing.

It seemed to the old man that the whole afternoon had stilled to watch his gesture of self-command, that even the leaves of the trees had stopped shaking.

140 Dry-eyed and calm, he let his hands fall to his sides and stood erect, staring up into the sky.

The cloud of shining silver birds flew up and up, with a shrill cleaving of wings, over the dark ploughed land and the darker belts of trees and the bright folds of grass, until they floated high in the sunlight, like a cloud of motes of dust.

145 They wheeled in a wide circle, tilting their wings so there was flash after flash of light, and one after another they dropped from the sunshine of the upper sky to shadow, one after another, returning to the shadowed earth over trees and grass and field, returning to the valley and the shelter of night.

The garden was all a fluster and a flurry of returning birds. Then silence, and the
150 sky was empty.

The old man turned, slowly, taking his time; he lifted his eyes to smile proudly down the garden at his granddaughter. She was staring at him. She did not smile. She was wide-eyed, and pale in the cold shadow, and he saw the tears run shivering off her face.

Your Shoes by Michèle Roberts

I thought I knew you as well as I know this house. No secret places, no hidey-holes, nothing in you I couldn't see. Now I realise how you kept yourself from me, how I didn't really know you at all.

5 You're not here any longer so how can I speak to you? You can't speak to someone who isn't there. Only mad people talk to an empty chest of drawers, a bed that hasn't been slept in for weeks. Someone half-mad, with grief that is, might pick up a shoe from the rug and hold it like a baby. Someone like me might do that. As if the shoe might still be warm or give a clue to where you've gone. One shoe pointed in fact towards the bedroom window, the view of the front
10 garden, and the other pointed towards the door. They wanted to get out, to get away, just like you did. I made them neat again, I stowed them in the wardrobe. Just in case. I locked the wardrobe door on those rebellious shoes. They could be like me and grieve in the darkness. For a bit. Then I let them out. I'm not cruel. But they've got to learn, haven't they. Kids these days. Well.

15 I can't send you a letter, either, because I don't know your address. There's no point really in writing this because it can't reach you. You have to live in a house with a front door and a letter-box if the postman is to deliver mail, and I don't suppose you do. It's not very likely, is it, you've found yourself a place. I don't know where you are. You just went off, just ran out of the house in the middle of
20 the night, and left me.

It costs me a lot to admit that, can't you understand? If I wrap my arms around myself and hold tight it keeps the pain in. Stops it spilling out and making a terrible mess. If I keep my mouth pursed tight I can't scream or throw up. If I imagine that you're gone for good, that you'll never come back, then this terrible
25 wailing sound will begin and never stop, I might go mad. At least this paper has ruled lines my writing can't fall off.

If you opened the door now and came in you'd find me here in your room. I'm lying curled up in the middle of the bed, on top of the duvet. I've drawn the curtains because the light hurts my eyes. It's already lunchtime but I don't want to
30 face the fridge, the freezer, the microwave. I'm not hungry. I'm better off here, looking at the locked wardrobe door. Your shoes are standing outside it now, side by side. The right shoe on the right-hand side and the left shoe on the left. In their proper places, no fuss, like a husband and wife. I'd like you to get married one day, I'd like you to have a normal life, of course I would. I've tied the shoes' laces
35 together so they won't get separated or lost. White laces, that I washed and ironed.

What did you have for lunch today? I hope you ate something. Did you beg for the money to buy a burger or a sandwich? I'd like to think you had a proper lunch. Something hot. Soup, perhaps, in a Styrofoam cup. You used to love tinned
40 tomato soup. Cream of. I always urged you to eat proper meals, meat and two veg or something salady, when you got home from school. You liked snacks better as you got older, it was the fashion amongst your friends I think, all day long you ate crisps and buns and I don't know what, at teatime when you came in you'd say you weren't hungry then late at night I'd catch you raiding the kitchen cupboards.
45 Fistfuls of currants and sultanas you'd jam into your mouth, one custard cream after another, you'd wolf all my supply of chocolate bars.

How do you feed yourself out there on the street? You're too young to get a job, who'd have you and what could you possibly do? What do you have to do to be fed? Do you have to go with men, is that it? How else could you get the money if you don't beg? There are so many of you begging for the money to buy food, stands to reason there isn't enough to go round. People don't like being continually asked, do they, they don't like being treated like bottomless pits. These days you have to choose who to give money to. I don't mean the starving millions in Africa, I mean the people of your age hanging about outside the supermarkets and the tube stations up in London, around the railway stations, I've seen the photos in the newspapers, it's not very nice having to imagine you mixing with people like that. Drug addicts and so on. You're fifteen years old. What do those men make you do? What do you have to do to get money for food?

Your father didn't mean it when he told you those things the other night. You've got to understand, he lost his temper and used some unfortunate expressions. At your age I'm sure I wouldn't have known the meaning of any of those words. As a young girl I'd have been hit if I used such language as I've heard you use. I was very old-fashioned. Square, they called it then. I grew up in a very old-fashioned family. Of course we had marvellous times together but my father was very strict. It didn't do me any harm. There was no truancy in our family in those days I can assure you, we simply wouldn't have dared. It was unthinkable. Not like you and your friends. We weren't spoilt. Not like your generation. These enormous presents at Christmas and so on. There wasn't the money. Your father works himself nearly to death for his family, for us. Because he loves us and wants us to have what he didn't. Little luxuries. What you and your lot take for granted. And me with my teaching job, I've done my bit for you too. We've given you everything a child could possibly want.

I'm sure you'd never have left if you realised I'd be this upset. You didn't mean to hurt me, did you. You never meant to make me so unhappy I'm sure. It was that mob you got in with at school. That Vanessa for instance. I wouldn't be surprised to hear she's on drugs. She had that look. You're so innocent, you didn't realise. You're too trusting, too kind, you don't know what these people can be like.

People pretend to be kind but they're ghouls. They ring up to see how I am and I can hear them gloat. It's not their fifteen-year-old daughter who's left home and gone off God knows where. The doctor's given me something to help me sleep and I've taken a week's sick leave from school. I try to put on a cheerful face. Oh, I say: she'll be back soon, I'm sure of it, why, she hasn't even taken her new shoes!

I don't think you have a clue how we feel. Just because we're not ones for letting it all out in public doesn't mean we don't live with this terrible pain. We don't speak of it much. But of course we know how each other feels. We have to be brave, we have to get on with living. The doctor told me: try to live from day to day. That's what they tell dying people too, I've heard it on a radio programme on hospices. You're not to die, d'you hear. You're alive somewhere aren't you. Sooner or later you'll ring up won't you from wherever you are. Some squat full of dropouts and drug addicts. Some cardboard box under a bridge. Some pile of filth. Of course they wouldn't have telephones there, I know that, you know what I mean. My daughter sleeping on a pile of filth I can't bear it.

You've got to understand. When your father called you a dirty slut he didn't mean you to take it personally. It was just a manner of speaking. In the heat of the moment. He adores you, you know that. It's just that he feels protective of you, and he can't stand being answered back. He can't stand rudeness. Not from you, not from anybody. What did you expect, being brought home drunk at three in the morning? We were half out of our minds with worry, of course we were upset. I've always thought of you as just an empty-headed blonde, I've never thought

100 you were really bad. Then I find out that you drink alcohol at parties and smoke
pot. Of course your father was angry. After all this is his house. You shouldn't
have got so upset. I'm sure he didn't mean all of what he said.

I dreamed of my mother last night. There was so much I wanted to say to her and
now it's too late. Daughters ought to be close to their mothers. I wasn't to mine.
105 She was a very stupid woman. She never had much of an education, then the war
came and she joined up. I've still got a photo of her in uniform. Blonde hair done
up in sausages on top of her head, cap stuck on one side, big lipsticked mouth. A
plump woman with a loud jolly laugh. Fat, let's be honest. Terribly vulgar, always
saying the wrong thing then laughing. My poor father used to wince. He shouldn't
110 have married her, he should have chosen someone more like himself. Then I
might have had a better childhood.

My mother was like you, she liked a drink. She used to do the housework with a
cigarette hanging out of her mouth, then she'd put her feet up and have a gin and
tonic. She was very clean, I'll give her that, she kept us and the house spotless.
115 She never had much time for me, I was just a girl, she preferred my brother. She
thought I should be a housewife like her but I surprised everybody by getting into
college to do domestic science. She brought me up to know how to fill bridge rolls
for parties, how to make Yorkshire pudding for Sunday lunch. Then I went ahead
of her and learned about nutritional science. Miss La-di-Da she used to call me. I
120 was thin, rather plain. I was fair like her, but my hair was straight. She had hers
dyed more and more golden. She had a bouffant perm. The face powder used to
collect in the creases of her cheeks and melt. Then she'd powder over it. She wore
a girdle to hold herself in. She lived her whole married life in a suburb in a
detached house with four bedrooms and she thought it was heaven. Well, she
125 would, after the semi-slum she grew up in up north. She was jealous because I
loved my father more than her. We'd go for walks in the park together. We talked
about things she couldn't understand.

It always hurt me, how nice she was to you. She spoiled you. She loved you more
than she loved me. It isn't fair. That was the cry of my girlhood. I had to help with
130 the housework but my brother did nothing. I was always racing to get done so I
could go out with my father. He took me to the golf club and introduced me to all
his friends. Once he took me to the pub. He told me I was bright and had a real
future ahead of me. I swore that when I grew up I wouldn't be like my mother.
Well at least I've kept my figure. I'm not fat like she was. She wore the most
135 unsuitable clothes. Always whatever was in fashion, regardless, she liked bright
colours, lots of costume jewellery, she looked a bit of a tart, let's face it, stiletto
heels, charm bracelets, the lot.

You've got small feet just like mine. Like hers. All the women in our family have
small feet. Sturdy, with a strong arch and short toes. For a couple of years now
140 I've been able to buy your shoes without having to drag you round the shops.
Moan whine, after ten minutes in Marks you'd threaten you were going to faint
and I had to get you out into the fresh air. They're lovely, these shoes I bought
you. White trainers, you see I know what you like. I thought you'd love them. I'm
looking after them for you. I've got them under the duvet with me now. I'm
145 keeping an eye on them, oh yes. They are perfect because they're new, they've
never been worn.

I had a white wedding. My father had been saving for it for years, he said nothing
was too good for his little girl. He gave me away, I walked down the aisle on his
arm feeling numb. I married your father on the rebound, everybody knew that I
150 was desperately in love with Pete, he was the great love of my life, when he went
off and left me I thought I might as well marry your father. He was always there
in the background, he'd been waiting for me. He's been a good husband, a good

father. Everyone said how lucky I was. Of course I never told my mother I wasn't a virgin, she'd have had fifty fits. My father would have killed me if he'd known.

155 Of course I wanted you. Of course I love you. It's hurtful and wicked to say I don't. I suppose it's my fault you've left home to sleep rough God knows where. Go on, blame your mother, everyone else does. I'm a failure as a mother. I didn't give you enough of whatever it was. You've always been very difficult. I did my best, what more could I do? Next thing you'll be saying it's because I didn't breastfeed you,
160 or because I didn't pick you up every time you cried. You can't imagine what it was like. At night you cried so much, in the end I used to shut the door on you and go back downstairs. I was exhausted. Your father slept through most of it, he said it wasn't his job. Just like my father. He wasn't interested in me when I was little, then when I was older and showed I had a brain, that was when he got
165 involved. Oh but we did have a lot of happy times too, I know we did. Don't forget that. I wish you wouldn't sulk. I wish you'd stop sulking and answer me.

It's cosy in here. Peaceful, too. I've unplugged the telephone so that I can concentrate on you and we shan't be disturbed. It'll be dark soon, the street lamps have just come on, I can see one shining through the curtains. Funny, you
170 never did like these curtains. I remember I got them in a sale up in town, I thought they were lovely, really modern with these splashes of white and grey, they were exactly what I'd have wanted as a girl. Then when you came home and saw what I'd done you flew into a temper, you said you wanted the old curtains back. By then it was too late, I'd thrown them away. I'd gone to so much trouble
175 to give you a surprise, I couldn't believe you'd be so ungrateful. Then you had to go and burst into floods of tears, that was the last straw, oh you used to be so unkind to me. Throwing my presents back in my face.

At first I kept the shoes in the box I made them pack them in at the shop, tenderly wrapped in tissue-paper. Delicate white sheets, rustling, uncreased. Then I tried
180 them in the wardrobe, then side by side on the rug. They're best in here with me I think, safe and warm in bed. Tucked up tight.

How could you do that to us. How could you. Boasting about it even. I think you wanted us to find out. Thank God I had the sense to look in your bag that night. You laughed at me, you said lots of girls in your class had had sex by the time
185 they were fifteen, you weren't going to be the exception.

After my mother died I had to clear out her clothes and pack them up for jumble. Her shoes hurt me so much. Rows of high-heels, all of them too small for her, she was so vain, all of them moulded to the shape of her poor feet. You could see how her toes were all bent over, misshapen. Bulges where she'd had bunions, corn-
190 plasters. Who'd have wanted them? I threw them all in the dustbin. Then on the way home I stopped the car and bought you a pair of new shoes as a surprise, really beautiful ones, the best I could afford.

Your father will be home soon. I've locked the bedroom door so that he can't get in. I want to be alone with you for a bit. My darling girl whom I love so much. I
195 hold you to my breast and rock you like my mother never rocked me. You're so small and pale. Let me hold you while you cry.

Laces like strings of white liquorice. They taste sweet.

There, my darling, there. You're at home with mother, everything's all right. I knew you'd come back, I knew you'd come back to me.

200 I love you I love you so much oh yes oh yes.

The Darkness
Out There by Penelope Lively

She walked through flowers, the girl, ox-eye daisies and vetch and cow parsley, keeping to the track at the edge of the field. She could see the cottage in the distance, shrugged down into the dip beyond the next hedge. 'Mrs Rutter,' Pat had said, 'Mrs Rutter at Nether Cottage, you don't know her, Sandra? She's a dear old
5   thing, all on her own, of course, we try to keep an eye. A wonky leg after her op. and the home help's off with a bad back this week. So could you make that your Saturday afternoon session, dear? Lovely. There'll be one of the others. I'm not sure who.'

Pat had a funny eye, a squint, so that her glance swerved away from you as she
10   talked. And a big chest jutting under washed-out jerseys. Are people who help other people always not very nice-looking? Very busy being busy; always in a rush. You didn't get people like Mrs Carpenter at the King's Arms running the Good Neighbours' Club. People with platinum highlights and spike-heel suede boots.

15   She looked down at her own legs, the girl, bare brown legs brushing through the grass, polleny summer grass that glinted in the sun.

She hoped it would be Susie, the other person. Or Liz. They could have a good giggle, doing the floors and that. Doing her washing, this old Mrs Rutter.

They were all in the Good Neighbours' Club, her set at school. Quite a few of the
20   boys, too. It had become a sort of craze, the thing to do. They were really nice, some of the old people. 'The old folks,' Pat called them. Pat had done the notice in the library: 'Come and have fun giving a helping hand to the old folks. Adopt a granny.' And the jokey cartoon drawing of a dear old bod with specs on the end of her nose and a shawl. One or two of the old people had been a bit sharp about
25   that.

The track followed the hedge round the field to the gate and the plank bridge over the stream. The dark reach of the spinney came right to the gate there so that she would have to walk by the edge of it with the light suddenly shutting off the bare wide sky of the field. Packer's End.

30   You didn't go by yourself through Packer's End if you could help it, not after tea-time, anyway. A German plane came down in the war and the aircrew were killed and there were people who'd heard them talking still, chattering in German on their radios, voices coming out of the trees, nasty, creepy. People said.

She kept to the track, walking in the flowers with corn running in the wind
35   between her and the spinney. She thought suddenly of blank-eyed helmeted heads, looking at you from among branches. She wouldn't go in there for a thousand pounds, not even in bright day like now, with nothing coming out of the dark slab of trees but bird song – blackbirds and thrushes and robins and that. It was a rank place, all whippy saplings and brambles and a gully with a dumped
40   mattress and bedstead and an old fridge. And, somewhere, presumably, the crumbling rusty scraps of metal and cloth and ... bones?

It was all right out here in the sunshine. Fine. She stopped to pick grass stems out of her sandal: she saw the neat print of the strap-marks against her sunburn, pink-white on brown. Somebody had said she had pretty feet, once: she looked at

45   them clean and plump and neat on the grass. A ladybird crawled across a toe.

    When they were small, six and seven and eight, they'd been scared stiff of Packer's End. Then, they hadn't known about the German plane. It was different things then; witches and wolves and tigers. Sometimes they'd go there for a dare, several of them, skittering over the field and into the edge of the trees, giggling
50   and shrieking, not too far in, just far enough for it to be scary, for the branch shapes to look like faces and clawed hands, for the wolves to rustle and creep in the greyness you couldn't quite see into, the clotted shifting depths of the place.

    But after, lying on your stomach at home on the hearth rug watching telly with the curtains drawn and the dark shut out, it was cosy to think of Packer's End, where
55   you weren't.

    After they were twelve or so the witches and wolves went away. Then it was the German plane. And other things too. You didn't know who there might be around, in woods and places. Like stories in the papers. Girl attacked on lonely road. Police hunt rapist. There was this girl, people at school said, this girl some time
60   back who'd been biking along the field path and these two blokes had come out of Packer's End. They'd had a knife, they'd threatened to carve her up, there wasn't anything she could do, she was at their mercy. People couldn't remember what her name was, exactly, she didn't live round here any more. Two enormous blokes, sort of gypsy types.

65   She put her sandal back on. She walked through the thicker grass by the hedge and felt it drag at her legs and thought of swimming in warm seas. She put her hand on the top of her head and her hair was hot from the sun, a dry burning cap. One day, this year, next year, sometime, she would go to places like on travel brochures and run into a blue sea. She would fall in love and she would get a
70   good job and she would have one of those new Singers that do zig-zag stitch and make an embroidered silk coat.

    One day.

    Now, she would go to this old Mrs Rutter's and have a bit of a giggle with Susie and come home for tea and wash her hair. She would walk like this through the
75   silken grass with the wind seething the corn and the secret invisible life of birds beside her in the hedge. She would pick a blue flower and examine its complexity of pattern and petal and wonder what it was called and drop it. She would plunge her face into the powdery plate of an elderflower and smell cat, tom-cat, and sneeze and scrub her nose with the back of her hand. She would hurry through
80   the gate and over the stream because that was a bit too close to Packer's End for comfort and she would ...

    He rose from the plough beyond the hedge.

    She screamed.

    'Christ!' she said, 'Kerry Stevens, you stupid so-and-so, what d'you want to go
85   and do that for, you give me the fright of my life.'

    He grinned. 'I seen you coming. Thought I might as well wait.'

    Not Susie. Not Liz either. Kerry Stevens from Richmond Way. Kerry Stevens that none of her lot reckoned much on, with his blacked licked-down hair and slitty eyes. Some people you only have to look at to know they're not up to much.

90   'Didn't know you were in the Good Neighbours.'

    He shrugged. They walked in silence. He took out an Aero bar, broke off a bit, offered it. She said, 'Oh, thanks.' They went chewing towards the cottage where old Mrs Rutter with her wonky leg would be ever so pleased to see them because they were really sweet, lots of the old people. Ever so grateful the old poppets was
95   what Pat said, not that you'd put it quite like that yourself.

'Just give it a push, the door. It sticks, see. That's it.'

She seemed composed of circles, a cottage-loaf of a woman, with a face below which chins collapsed one into another, a creamy smiling pool of a face in which her eyes snapped and darted.

100 'Tea, my duck?' she said. 'Tea for the both of you? I'll put us a kettle on.'

The room was stuffy. It had a gaudy lino floor with the pattern rubbed away in front of the sink and round the table; the walls were cluttered with old calendars and pictures torn from magazines; there was a smell of cabbage. The alcove by the fireplace was filled with china ornaments: big-eyed flop-eared rabbits and
105 beribboned kittens and flowery milkmaids and a pair of naked chubby children wearing daisy chains.

The woman hauled herself from a sagging armchair. She glittered at them from the stove, manoeuvring cups, propping herself against the draining-board. 'What's your names, then? Sandra and Kerry. Well, you're a pretty girl, Sandra,
110 aren't you. Pretty as they come. There was – let me see, who was it? – Susie, last week. That's right, Susie.' Her eyes investigated, quick as mice. 'Put your jacket on the back of the door, dear, you won't want to get that messy. Still at school, are you?'

The boy said, 'I'm leaving, July. They're taking me on at the garage, the Blue Star.
115 I been helping out there on and off, before.'

Mrs Rutter's smiles folded into one another. Above them, her eyes examined him. 'Well, I expect that's good steady money if you'd nothing special in mind. Sugar?'

There was a view from the window out over a bedraggled garden with the stumps of spent vegetables and a matted flower-bed and a square of shaggy grass.
120 Beyond, the spinney reached up to the fence, a no-man's-land of willow herb and thistle and small trees, growing thicker and higher into the full density of woodland. Mrs Rutter said, 'Yes, you have a look out, aren't I lucky – right up beside the wood. Lovely it is in the spring, the primroses and that. Mind, there's not as many as there used to be.'

125 The girl said, 'Have you lived here for a long time?'

'Most of my life, dear. I came here as a young married woman, and that's a long way back, I can tell you. You'll be courting before long yourself, I don't doubt. Like bees round the honeypot, they'll be.'

The girl blushed. She looked at the floor, at her own feet, neat and slim and
130 brown. She touched, secretly, the soft skin of her thigh; she felt her breasts poke up and out at the thin stuff of her top; she licked the inside of her teeth, that had only the one filling, a speck like a pin-head. She wished there was Susie to have a giggle with, not just that Kerry Stevens.

The boy said, 'What'd you like us to do?'

135 His chin was explosive with acne; at his middle, his jeans yawned from his T-shirt, showing pale chilly flesh. Mrs Rutter said, 'I expect you're a nice strong boy, aren't you? I daresay you'd like to have a go at the grass with the old mower. Sandra can give this room a do, that would be nice. It's as much as I can manage to have a dust of the ornaments just now, I can't get down to the floor.'

140 When he had gone outside the girl fetched broom and mop and dustpan from a cupboard under the narrow stair. The cupboard, stacked with yellowing newspapers, smelt of damp and mouse. When she returned, the old woman was back in the armchair, a composite chintzy mass from which cushions oozed and her voice flowed softly on. 'That's it, dear, you just work round, give the corners a
145 brush if you don't mind, that's where the dust settles. Mind your pretty skirt, pull it up a bit, there's only me to see if you're showing a bit of bum. That's ever such

a nice style. I expect your mum made it, did she?'

The girl said, 'Actually I did.'

'Well now, fancy! You're a little dressmaker, too, are you? I was good with my
needle when I was younger, my eyesight's past it now, of course. I made my own
wedding dress, ivory silk with lace insets. A Vogue pattern it was, with a
sweetheart neckline.'

The door opened. Kerry said, 'Where'll I put the clippings?'

'There's the compost heap down the bottom, by the fence. And while you're down
there could you get some sticks from the wood for kindling, there's a good lad.'

When he had gone she went on. 'That's a nice boy. It's a pity they put that stuff on
their hair these days, sticky-looking. I expect you've got lots of boyfriends, though,
haven't you?'

The girl poked in a crack at a clump of fluff. 'I don't really know Kerry that much.'

'Don't you, dear? Well, I expect you get all sorts, in your club thing, the club that
Miss Hammond runs.'

'The Good Neighbours, Pat, we call her.'

'She was down here last week. Ever such a nice person. Kind. It's sad she never
married.'

The girl said, 'Is that your husband in the photo, Mrs Rutter?'

'That's right, dear. In his uniform. The Ox and Bucks. After he got his stripes. He
was a lovely man.'

She sat back on her heels, the dustpan on her lap. The photo was yellowish, in a
silver frame. 'Did he...?'

'Killed in the war, dear. Right at the start. He was in one of the first campaigns, in
Belgium, and he never came back.'

The girl saw a man with a tooth-brush moustache, his army cap slicing his
forehead. 'That's terrible.'

'Tragic. There was a lot of tragedies in the war. It's nice it won't be like that for
you young people nowadays. Touch wood, cross fingers. I like young people, I
never had any children, it's been a loss, that, I've got a sympathy with young
people.'

The girl emptied the dustpan into the bin outside the back door. Beyond the fence,
she could see the bushes thrash and Kerry's head bob among them. She thought,
rather him than me, but it's different for boys, for him anyway, he's not a nervy
type, it's if you're nervy you get bothered about things like Packer's End.

She was nervy, she knew. Mum always said so.

Mrs Rutter was rummaging in a cupboard by her chair. 'Chocky? I always keep a
few chockies by for visitors.' She brought out a flowered tin. 'There. Do you know,
I've had this twenty years, all but. Look at the little cornflowers. And the daisies.
They're almost real, aren't they?'

'Sweet,' said the girl.

'Take them out and see if what's-'s-name would like one?'

There was a cindery path down the garden, ending at a compost heap where
eggshells gleamed among the leaves and grass clippings. Rags of plastic fluttered
from sticks in a bed of cabbages. The girl picked her way daintily, her toes
wincing against the cinders. A place in the country. One day she would have a
place in the country, but not like this. Sometime. A little white house peeping over
a hill, with a stream at the bottom of a crisp green lawn and an orchard with old

apple trees and a brown pony. And she would walk in the long grass in this orchard in a straw hat with these two children, a boy and a girl, children with fair shiny hair like hers, and there'd be this man.

She leaned over the fence and shouted, 'Hey ...'

'What?'

She brandished the box.

He came up, dumping an armful of sticks. 'What's this for, then?'

'She said. Help yourself.'

He fished among the sweets, his fingers etched with dirt. 'I did a job on your dad's car last week. That blue Escort's his, isn't it?'

'Mm.'

'July, I'll be starting full-time. When old Bill retires. With day-release at the tech.'

She thought of oily workshop floors, of the fetid underside of cars. She couldn't stand the feel of dirt; if her hands were the least grubby she had to go and wash; a rim of grime under her nails could make her shudder. She said, 'I don't know how you can, all that muck.'

He fished for another chocolate. 'Nothing wrong with a bit of dirt. What you going to do, then?'

'Secretarial.'

Men didn't mind so much. At home, her dad did things like unblocking the sink and cleaning the stove; Mum was the same as her, just the feel of grease and stuff made her squirm. They couldn't either of them wear anything that had a stain or a spot.

He said, 'I don't go much on her.'

'Who?'

He waved towards the cottage.

'She's all right. What's wrong with her, then?'

He shrugged. 'I dunno. The way she talks and that.'

'She lost her husband,' said the girl. 'In the war.' She considered him, across the fence, over a chasm. Mum said boys matured later, in many ways.

'There's lots of people done that.'

She looked beyond him, into distances. 'Tragic, actually. Well, I'll go back and get on. She says can you see to her bins when you've got the sticks. She wants them carried down for the dustmen.'

Mrs Rutter watched her come in, glinting from the cushions.

'That's a good girl. Put the tin back in the cupboard, dear.'

'What would you like me to do now?'

'There's my little bit of washing by the sink. Just the personal things to rinse through. That would be ever so kind.'

The girl ran water into the basin. She measured in the soap-flakes. She squeezed the pastel nylons, the floating sinuous tights. 'It's a lovely colour, that turquoise.'

'My niece got me that last Christmas. Nightie and a little jacket to go. I was telling you about my wedding dress. The material came from Macy's, eight yards. I cut it on the cross, for the hang. Of course, I had a figure then.' She heaved herself round in the chair. 'You're a lovely shape, Sandra. You take care you stay that way.'

'I can get a spare tyre,' the girl said. 'If I'm not careful.'

Outside, the bin lids rattled.

'I hope he's minding my edging. I've got lobelia planted out along that path.'

'I love blue flowers.'

245 'You should see the wood in the spring, with the bluebells. There's a place right far in where you get lots coming up still. I used to go in there picking every year before my leg started playing me up. Jugs and jugs of them, for the scent. Haven't you ever seen them?'

The girl shook her head. She wrung out the clothes, gathered up the damp skein.
250 'I'll put these on the line, shall I?'

When she returned the boy was bringing in the filled coal-scuttle and a bundle of sticks.

'That's it,' said Mrs Rutter. 'Under the sink, that's where they go. You'll want to have a wash after that, won't you. Put the kettle on, Sandra, and we'll top up the
255 pot.'

The boy ran his hands under the tap. His shirt clung to his shoulder blades, damp with sweat. He looked over the bottles of detergent, the jug of parsley, the handful of flowers tucked into a Coronation mug. He said, 'Is that the wood where there was that German plane came down in the war?'

260 'Don't start on that,' said the girl. 'It always gives me the willies.'

'What for?'

'Scary.'

The old woman reached forward and prodded the fire. 'Put a bit of coal on for me, there's a good boy. What's to be scared of? It's over and done with, good
265 riddance to bad rubbish.'

'It was there, then?'

'Shut up,' said the girl.

'Were you here?'

'Fill my cup up, dear, would you. I was here. Me and my sister. My sister Dot.
270 She's dead now, two years. Heart. That was before she was married of course, nineteen forty-two, it was.'

'Did you see it come down?'

She chuckled. 'I saw it come down all right.'

'What was it?' said the boy. 'Messerschmitt?'

275 'How would I know that, dear? I don't know anything about aeroplanes. Anyway, it was all smashed up by the time I saw it, you couldn't have told t'other from which.'

The girl's hand hovered, the tea-cup halfway to her mouth. She sipped, put it down. 'You saw it? Ooh, I wouldn't have gone anywhere near.'

280 'It would have been burning,' said the boy. 'It'd have gone up in flames.'

'There weren't any flames; it was just stuck there in the ground, end up, with mess everywhere. Drop more milk, dear, if you don't mind.'

The girl shuddered. 'I s'pose they'd taken the bodies away by then.'

Mrs Rutter picked out a tea-leaf with the tip of the spoon. She drank, patted the
285 corner of her mouth delicately with a tissue. 'No, no, 'course not. There was no one else seen it come down. We'd heard the engine and you could tell there was

trouble, the noise wasn't right, and we looked out and saw it come down smack in the trees. 'Course we hadn't the telephone so there was no ringing the police or the Warden at Clapton. Dot said we should maybe bike to the village but it was a filthy wet night, pouring cats and dogs, and fog, too, and we didn't know if it was one of ours or one of theirs, did we? So Dot said better go and have a look first.'

'But either way ...' the boy began.

'We got our wellies on, and Dot had the big lantern, and we went off. It wasn't very far in. We found it quite quick and Dot grabbed hold of me and pointed and we saw one of the wings sticking up with the markings on and we knew it was one of theirs. We cheered, I can tell you.'

The boy stared at her over the rim of the cup, blank-faced.

'Dot said bang goes some more of the bastards, come on let's get back into the warm and we just started back when we heard this noise.'

'Noise?'

'Sort of a moaning.'

'Oh,' cried the girl. 'How awful, weren't they ...'

'So we got up closer and Dot held the lantern so we could see and there was three of them, two in the front and they were dead, you could see that all right, one of them had his ...'

The girl grimaced. 'Don't.'

Mrs Rutter's chins shook, the pink and creamy chins. 'Good job you weren't there then, my duck. Not that we were laughing at the time, I can tell you, rain teeming down and a raw November night, and that sight under our noses. It wasn't pretty but I've never been squeamish, nor Dot neither. And then we saw the other one.'

'The other one?' said the boy warily.

'The one at the back. He was trapped, see, the way the plane had broken up. There wasn't any way he could get out.'

The girl stiffened. 'Oh, lor, you mean he ...'

'He was hurt pretty bad. He was kind of talking to himself. Something about mutter, mutter ... Dot said he's not going to last long, and a good job too, three of them that'll be. She'd been a VAD so she knew a bit about casualties, see.'
Mrs Rutter licked her lips; she looked across at them, her eyes darting. 'Then we went back to the cottage.'

There was silence. The fire gave a heave and a sigh. 'You what?' said the boy.

'Went back inside. It was bucketing down, cats and dogs.'

The boy and girl sat quite still, on the far side of the table. 'That was eighteen months or so after my hubby didn't come back from Belgium.' Her eyes were on the girl; the girl looked away.

'Tit for tat, I said to Dot.'

After a moment she went on. 'Next morning it was still raining and blow me if the bike hadn't got a puncture. I said to Dot I'm not walking to the village in this, and that's flat, and Dot was running a bit of a temp, she had the flu or something coming on. I tucked her up warm and when I'd done the chores I went back in the wood, to have another look. He must have been a tough so-and-so, that jerry, he was still mumbling away. It gave me a turn, I can tell you. I'd never imagined he'd last the night. I could see him better, in the day-time; he was bashed up pretty nasty. I'd thought he was an old bloke, too, but he wasn't. He'd have been twentyish, that sort of age.'

335 The boy's spoon clattered to the floor; he did not move.

'I reckon he may have seen me, not that he was in a state to take much in. He called out something. I thought, oh no, you had this coming to you, mate, there's a war on. You won't know that expression – it was what everybody said in those days. I thought, why should I do anything for you? Nobody did anything for my
340 Bill, did they? I was a widow at thirty-nine. I've been on my own ever since.'

The boy shoved his chair back from the table.

'He must have been a tough bastard, like I said. He was still there that evening, but the next morning he was dead. The weather'd perked up by then and I walked to the village and got a message to the people at Clapton. They were ever
345 so surprised; they didn't know there'd been a jerry plane come down in the area at all. There were lots of people came to take bits for souvenirs. I had a bit myself but it's got mislaid, you tend to mislay things when you get to my age.'

The boy had got up. He glanced down at the girl. 'I'm going,' he said. 'Dunno about you, but I'm going.'

350 She stared at the lacy cloth on the table, the fluted china cup. 'I'll come too.'

'Eh?' said the old woman. 'You're off, are you? That was nice of you to see to my little jobs for me. Tell what's-'er-name to send someone next week if she can. I like having someone young about the place, once in a while. I've got a sympathy with young people. Here – you're forgetting your pretty jacket, Sandra, what's the
355 hurry? 'Bye then, my ducks, see you close my gate, won't you?'

The boy walked ahead, fast; the girl pattered behind him, sliding on the dry grass. At the gateway into the cornfield he stopped. He said, not looking at her, looking towards the furzy edge of the wood, 'Christ!'

The wood sat there in the afternoon sun. Wind stirred the trees. Birds sang.
360 There were not, the girl realised, wolves or witches or tigers. Nor were there prowling blokes, gypsy-type blokes. And there were not chattering ghostly voices. Somewhere there were some scraps of metal overlooked by people hunting for souvenirs.

The boy said, 'I'm not going near that old bitch again.' He leaned against the gate,
365 clenching his fists on an iron rung; he shook slightly. 'I won't ever forget him, that poor sod.'

She nodded.

'Two bloody nights. Christ!'

And she would hear, she thought, always, for a long time anyway, that voice
370 trickling on, that soft old woman's voice: would see a tin painted with cornflowers, pretty china ornaments.

'It makes you want to throw up,' he said. 'Someone like that.'

She couldn't think of anything to say. He had grown; he had got older and larger. His anger eclipsed his acne, the patches of grease on his jeans, his lardy midriff.
375 You could get people all wrong, she realised with alarm. You could get people wrong and there was a darkness that was not the darkness of tree shadows and murky undergrowth and you could not draw the curtains and keep it out because it was in your head, once known, in your head for ever like lines from a song. One moment you were walking in long grass with the sun on your hair and birds
380 singing and the next you glimpsed darkness, an inescapable darkness. The darkness was out there and it was a part of you and you would never be without it, ever.

She walked behind him, through a world grown unreliable, in which flowers sparkle and birds sing but everything is not as it appears, oh no.

The Genius by Frank O'Connor

Some kids are cissies by nature but I was a cissy by conviction. Mother had told me about geniuses; I wanted to be one, and I could see for myself that fighting, as well as being sinful, was dangerous. The kids round the Barrack where I lived were always fighting. Mother said they were savages, that I needed proper

5 friends, and that once I was old enough to go to school I would meet them.

My way, when someone wanted to fight and I could not get away, was to climb on the nearest wall and argue like hell in a shrill voice about Our Blessed Lord and good manners. This was a way of attracting attention, and it usually worked because the enemy, having stared incredulously at me for several minutes,

10 wondering if he would have time to hammer my head on the pavement before someone came out to him, yelled something like 'blooming cissy' and went away in disgust. I didn't like being called a cissy but I preferred it to fighting. I felt very like one of those poor mongrels who slunk through our neighbourhood and took to their heels when anyone came near them, and I always tried to make friends

15 with them.

I toyed with games, and enjoyed kicking a ball gently before me along the pavement till I discovered that any boy who joined me grew violent and started to shoulder me out of the way. I preferred little girls because they didn't fight so much, but otherwise I found them insipid and lacking in any solid basis of

20 information. The only women I cared for were grown-ups, and my most intimate friend was an old washerwoman called Miss Cooney who had been in the lunatic asylum and was very religious. It was she who had told me all about dogs. She would run a mile after anyone she saw hurting an animal, and even went to the police about them, but the police knew she was mad and paid no attention.

25 She was a sad-looking woman with grey hair, high cheekbones and toothless gums. While she ironed, I would sit for hours in the hot, steaming, damp kitchen, turning over the pages of her religious books. She was fond of me too, and told me she was sure I would be a priest. I agreed that I might be a bishop, but she didn't seem to think so highly of bishops. I told her there were so many other

30 things I might be that I couldn't make up my mind, but she only smiled at this. Miss Cooney thought there was only one thing a genius could be and that was a priest.

On the whole I thought an explorer was what I would be. Our house was in a square between two roads, one terraced above the other, and I could leave home,

35 follow the upper road for a mile past the Barrack, turn left on any of the intervening roads and lanes, and return almost without leaving the pavement. It was astonishing what valuable information you could pick up on a trip like that. When I came home I wrote down my adventures in a book called *The Voyages of Johnson Martin*, 'with many Maps and Illustrations, Irishtown University Press,

40 3s. 6d. nett'. I was also compiling *The Irishtown University Song Book for Use in Schools and Institutions by Johnson Martin*, which had the words and music of my favourite songs. I could not read music yet but I copied it from anything that came handy, preferring staff to solfa because it looked better on the page. But I still wasn't sure what I would be. All I knew was that I intended to be famous and

45 have a statue put up to me near that of Father Matthew, in Patrick Street. Father Matthew was called the Apostle of Temperance, but I didn't think much of temperance. So far our town hadn't a proper genius and I intended to supply the deficiency.

Tasks 1, 2, 3 and 4 ask for very specific references to the passages and the candidate has written the answers briefly and has kept to the point.

- There are key words in the quotation which the candidate has recognised. The most important of these is "strange". It is strange because the writer saw so much more of his mother than his father.

- The questions ask about attitudes and attitudes always leave some room for opinion. The candidate here has clearly thought carefully and has expressed his views carefully, taking details from the passage to justify what he says. It is a good answer to 2 and similarly to 3.

- Humour is always quite a difficult thing to deal with. The candidate has chosen the three examples of humour with care and has explained with some sympathy how humour helps to understand the characters.

- The last question, and there is a choice, gives a chance to use one's imagination and to develop personal ideas using either the passage or the poem as a starting point. This candidate has chosen to write a poem and has tried to make a member of his family real and amusing. He has also tried to add a little humour in much the same way as the original. The poem has a form and style suitable to its purpose so that it brings the character to life.

As we have already mentioned, often in English exams you are given a passage of literature or a poem to read and then asked to write in an imaginative way using what you have read as a starting point.

LITERARY STIMULUS

In this case you are going to be given a question which simply asks you to develop a piece of your own writing based on an idea or a theme in the original passage.

You are asked to read an extract from a novel, *A Portrait of the Artist as a Young Man* by James Joyce. This is a well known passage about a young boy receiving a beating at the hands of a cruel teacher. The setting is a religious school in Ireland. The task set at the end of the passage asks you, in a rather general way, to write about an incident involving a teacher and a pupil.

First read the passage, then look at the writing task and consider the options open to you. An example of writing is given.

To set the scene – the Prefect of Studies, Father Dolan, has visited the classroom of Father Arnall. A severe disciplinarian, he has already beaten one boy in the class for doing badly in his Latin grammar. In this passage he turns his attention to Stephen Dedalus, the central character in the story.

STIMULUS MATERIAL

> – You, boy, who are you?
> Stephen's heart jumped suddenly.
> – Dedalus, sir.
> – Why are you not writing like the others?
> – I… my…
> He could not speak with fright.
> – Why is he not writing, Father Arnall?
> – He broke his glasses, said Father Arnall, and I exempted him from work.
> – Broke? What is this I hear? What is this your name is? said the prefect of studies.
> – Dedalus, sir.
> – Out here, Dedalus. Lazy little schemer. I see schemer in your face. Where did you break your glasses?
> Stephen stumbled into the middle of the class, blinded by fear and haste.
> – Where did you break your glasses? repeated the prefect of studies.
> – The cinderpath, sir.
> – Hoho! The cinderpath! cried the prefect of studies. I know that trick.

Stephen lifted his eyes in wonder and saw for a moment Father Dolan's whitegrey not young face, his baldy whitegrey head with fluff at the sides of it, the steel rims of his spectacles and his nocoloured eyes looking through the glasses. Why did he say he knew that trick?

– Lazy idle little loafer! cried the prefect of studies. Broke my glasses! An old schoolboy trick. Out with your hand this moment!

Stephen closed his eyes and held out in the air his trembling hand with the palm upwards. He felt the prefect of studies touch it for a moment at the fingers to straighten it and then the swish of the sleeve of the soutane as the pandybat was lifted to strike. A hot burning stinging tingling blow like the loud crack of a broken stick made his trembling hand crumple together like a leaf in the fire; and at the sound and the pain scalding tears were driven into his eyes. His whole body was shaking with fright, his arm was shaking and his crumpled burning livid hand shook like a loose leaf in the air. A cry sprang to his lips, a prayer to be let off. But though the tears scalded his eyes and his limbs quivered with pain and fright he held back the hot tears and the cry that scalded his throat.

– Other hand! shouted the prefect of studies.

(N.B. James Joyce was a writer who experimented with his writing by not using speech marks for direct speech. You are advised to use speech marks in your writing. You can remind yourself of the use of speech marks by consulting p8.)

TASK Write about an incident involving a teacher and a pupil.

Examiner's tip Notice, as in this case here, that you are often not given very precise instructions for an imaginative writing task. One of the skills you must use is to interpret the question and see if you can think of an original idea. You are sometimes given some extra guidance which, in this case might be as follows:

"You could write about an imagined event as part of a story or, if you prefer, you could write about a real event."

How can you help yourself to make a decision about what to write? Firstly, check that you have clearly understood the wording in the task. Here, "Write about an incident involving a teacher and a pupil" gives you a wide choice. You are certainly not restricted to writing about a school teacher and school pupil – there are literally hundreds of other possibilities, and you might please an examiner by coming up with an original idea!

Read the example of writing in response to this task. You will see that this pupil appears not to use the story as a starting point at all. His writing suggests that he has interpreted the task very differently. However, if you look closely at his plan, you can begin to see links. He has in fact used a theme of physical punishment and turned it into a very different sort of story.

Before reading it though, let us think about how it might have been planned.

PLANNING ## What is involved in planning?

Planning can give you an initial idea; it can provide you with a shape or structure to your writing and it can allow you to think about possible scenes for description.

You will know what sorts of plans you feel comfortable with. Some students prefer to plan in a diagram, such as a spider diagram. Others prefer to write lists of events and ideas. Or you can "think aloud" with your writing – quickly jotting down all the ideas as they occur to you.

What is the link between a plan and the writing?

The purpose of a good plan is not to give you every idea or every word of your work! It is more to start you off and give you confidence. Think of it like a skeleton; your writing can then put all the flesh onto the bones.

One word of warning! Do not become a slave to the plan. Change your ideas as you see new possibilities, whilst you are writing. Here are three types of plan which could be used for the writing on pp38–9:

1 DIAGRAMMATIC

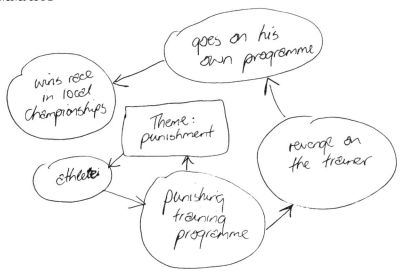

2 A LIST

- punishment
- theme of punishment in athletics
- boy being trained by cruel trainer
- revenge against trainer
- wins competition

3 "THINKING ALOUD"

I can see a boy who is an athlete and he is being overtrained by a harsh trainer who because he was injured wants the boy to win but he really wants to win for himself – the boy rejects the trainer and trains himself – this leads to an ending where the boy wins, the trainer sees this at the championships

"Write Imaginatively about an incident involving a teacher and a pupil."

"Run faster, boy! You're not trying," bellowed Mr. Graham.

Mark was running 1500m in his twice-weekly lunchtime training session for the forthcoming regional Junior Athletics Championship. Mr. Graham had agreed to take him on and train him. A tall, powerfully built former athlete, Mr. Graham never seemed satisfied with any of his pupils' achievements. His own athletic career had sadly been cut short when he badly broke his leg falling down some steps. As a result of this he now walked with a kind of sideways limp that made him look like he was not totally balanced all of the time.

"Come on Mark, you're not putting in any effort! Don't you want me to enter you for the Junior Athletics Championship?"

Mark crossed the finish line and sat down, exhausted, on the rubber track.

"I was trying, sir. It's my ankle, sir. It's gone all stiff," complained Mark between breaths. He thought this injury was probably because of Mr. Graham's insistence that he ran 1500 metres at least six times a week.

"Get back onto the track, Mark. You'll only get better with practice." Mr. Graham was a great believer in those old sayings.

"Can't I have a break please? I've been running all lunchtime. Surely I'm fast enough to enter the Championship now!" Mark knew that his time was around the level needed for entry, but to win he needed something extra.

"I give up! You just do not have the right attitude for athletics. You can enter the championship if you like, but I'm not training you anymore! You should know by now that pride comes between a fall." or before?!"

Mr. Graham walked off as briskly as his ankle would allow, leaving Mark sitting on the track, his head in his hands.

Mark vowed to himself that he would enter the Junior Athletic championship and he would win the 1500 metres, just to show Mr. Graham that he was wrong to not believe in his ability. He told himself that he would design a training schedule that he felt happy with. He would make use of the two weeks before the Championship to maximise his potential.

That evening he set about his new training system.

He had decided that varying the type of running would be more likely to improve his chances of winning than the intensive 1500 metre work demanded of him by Mr. Graham. He sent off the entry form for the championship by first class post and waited anxiously for the reply to be sent back, showing if he had fulfilled the entry requirements. This came back satisfactorily and the rest of the two weeks passed very quickly.

On the morning of the Championship, Mark was up early to perform his stretching exercises. His father drove him to the nearby athletics ground. He warmed up, then his first heat was called onto the track. Mark walked out nervously, worried whether going it alone was the right decision, after all, Mr. Graham was an ex-athlete himself. If Mark did not win this heat, he could not get into the final, and Mr. Graham would have achieved victory over him.

The race was actually just a formality. Mark won by ten seconds, so went on to the semi-final. This time, though, he was not so lucky. Three of the racers crossed the line at the same time. The result had to go to the judges for adjudication. While Mark was waiting, he saw an old car pull up and a man limp out to join the crowd. Mark's name rang out over the public address system in the list of finalists. Mr. Graham presented him with the gold certificate.

Examiner's commentary   This pupil has achieved a strong sense of character, for both the athlete and the trainer. This has been achieved through the use of dialogue which is used mainly to define the characters. Also, attention is paid to the key relationship between the two characters.

There is considerable variety in the way that the writing is structured. As readers we move from the dialogue during the training session, to a glimpse of Mr Graham's past, when we learn about his accident, then the point where Mark ("that evening") sends off his entry form for the championships, and finally we are brought to the day of the championships when Mr Graham comes back into the story. In fact, the plot is organised in such a way that the reader follows the experiences of the main character to the point where his problems are resolved by a deliberately constructed ending.

There is a good effort to achieve a number of themes in the writing: the punishment in the training schedule at the start; the over zealous enthusiasm of Mr Graham, in the hope that his pupil can be triumphant in his place; and then the themes of rejection, perseverance and triumph towards the end.

There is variety in the sentence structure, much of which is complex. This is an important skill – the ability to write in sentences which cover a number of points through linked or contrasting phrases. There is correct use of tenses in the use of verbs, and a number of effective adjectives and adverbs are also used. The punctuation and paragraphing, two other key skills, are also accurate.

Above all, the pupil is clearly in control of his ideas here and this gives the story a sense of progression. This may have been the result of careful planning.

MEDIA STIMULUS

The next few pages contain examples of stimulus material taken from media sources. Think about how the style of writing, and the vocabulary, differs from the stimulus material taken from literature.

STIMULUS MATERIAL

Mysterious Fireball Blasts Siberia

Cause remains unknown to this day

***From out of the blue**, an unidentified extraterrestial object leveled some 25 square miles of forest in remote Siberia early in this century. Giant 30-inch thick trees were snapped in two like mere matchsticks, creating an unparalleled, eerie scene of desolation shown in the contemporary photograph shown above.*

Something arrived from outer space on the morning of June 30, 1908, and exploded over the forests of central Siberia in a blinding flash, packing an incredibly destructive wallop. That much is certain. The powerful blast is estimated to have been equal to the detonation of 30 million tons of TNT. But the cause is still a matter of speculation.

The fact that a disaster had even taken place went unnoticed by most of the world. Remote and locked in the icy grip of winter for eight months of the year, the area where the blast occurred was largely uninhabited except for a scattering of the reindeer-herding Tungus people. So, despite the widespread devastation, there were no known human fatalities.

Stories of the cataclysm appeared only in regional newspapers. According to one reporter, "a heavenly body of fiery appearance cut across the sky… Neither its size nor shape could be made out, owing to its speed and unexpectedness. However, many people in different villages distinctly saw that when the flying object touched the horizon a huge flame shot up that cut the sky in two." Fearful sounds of the explosion filled the air, and violent tremors shook the land. "One had the impression that the earth was about to gape open and everything would be swallowed up in the abyss," he added, concluding that "the invisibility of the source inspired a kind of superstitious terror."

That very evening saw the onset of a series of strange "bright nights" throughout the Northern Hemisphere. One man in Russia discovered that he could take outdoor photographs at midnight; another reported: "I myself was aroused from sleep at 1:15, and so strong was the light at this hour, that I could read a book by it in my chamber quite comfortably.

At 1:45 the whole sky… was a delicate salmon pink."

Although the bright nights continued for about two months, no one linked them to the exploding fireball. Some reports speculated that they were unusually brilliant displays of the aurora borealis, although the flickering characteristic of such displays was missing. Only in 1930 did a British meteorologist conclude that the millions of tons of atmospheric dust from the Tunguska blast had acted as a vast solar reflector that illuminated the night skies.

Even that long-delayed connection might not have been made, however, had it not been for a young Russian scientist named Leonid A. Kulik. In 1921 the Russian Academy of Sciences assigned him the job of collecting information about meteorites. Just as he was about to embark on an exploratory trip to Siberia, a colleague handed him a 1908 newspaper clipping about passengers on the Trans-Siberian Railroad who claimed to have witnessed the fall of a large meteor. But Kulik could do little more than plot the presumed location of the impact before an early winter sealed access to the region. Years passed before he was able to arrange a second expedition.

In 1927, however, with a local Tungus man as his guide, Kulik made his way into the area of destruction. "I cannot really take in the whole majestic picture," he wrote in his diary. "From our observation point no sign of forest can be seen, for everything has been devastated and burned."

During the following weeks Kulik penetrated farther into the zone of devastation, expecting to find the remnants of a massive meteorite. What he found, much to his surprise, was an area near the very centre of the destruction where the trees were stripped bare of branches but still standing. The explosion evidently had taken place directly above the trees, killing them but leaving them upright.

Extensive exploration on subsequent expeditions convinced Kulik that he would discover neither meteorite nor crater. Although he had not come up with a satisfactory explanation for what had happened, he had succeeded in focusing the attention of other scientists on the mysterious cataclysm in far-off Siberia.

Since his day, an astounding array of theories has been offered to explain the devastation. Among the most exotic is the suggestion that it was caused by a nuclear explosion aboard an alien spaceship. Two other proposals require equal leaps of the imagination. One holds that a miniature black hole, perhaps no bigger than a speck of dust, struck the earth at Tunguska, passed all the way through the planet, and came out in the North Atlantic. Black holes are formed when ageing stars collapse into themselves and their gravity becomes so intense that not even rays of light can escape their pull. Passing through the earth, a black hole theoretically could set off shock waves powerful enough to devastate a forest.

The second theory attributes the damage to an interstellar lump of antimatter that fell to earth. Antimatter is, in effect, the mirror image of ordinary matter and carries an opposite electrical charge. When a particle of antimatter encounters a corresponding particle of matter, both are annihilated in a tremendous burst of energy, such as the explosion that occurred in Siberia.

A more widely accepted explanation says that the culprit was the head of a comet on a collision course with our planet. Plummeting toward the earth, it could have exploded in midair from the incredible heat produced by its friction with the atmosphere. But other scientists prefer a variant of Kulik's original hypothesis: that the Tunguska fireball was caused by a stony meteor or, more likely, an asteroid that exploded two or three miles above the earth, with heat so intense that the entire object was vaporized and the region below it was devastated.

Whatever the cause, whether comet or asteroid or some as yet undreamed-of intergalactic wanderer, the object certainly came from outer space. Recent analysis of microscopic particles apparently left by the explosion has demonstrated, from their content of the heavy metal iridium and other materials, that they are extraterrestrial in origin. Concurrent analysis of ice that was laid down in Antarctica in 1908 and 1909 revealed an exceptional accumulation of cosmic iridium; presumably it fell from the dust thrown into the stratosphere by the Tunguska blast. Based on the amounts of iridium found in Antarctica, the exploding object is estimated to have weighed a staggering 7 million tons.

The mystery of the Siberian fireball may never be resolved. But it does provide some food for thought. What if such an event were to occur again? And what if next time the blast took place not over the trackless wastes of Siberia but over some global trouble spot? Might a nervous nation, believing it was under nuclear attack, react in kind and push the whole world over the brink into the final holocaust? The prospect, to say the least, is sobering.

Monster in Lake Nyos

A freak of nature takes a devastating toll in Cameroon

Possibly a thousand years before the West African colony of Cameroon finally achieved independence in 1961, a silent invisible monster had begun to grow in the 600-foot depths of mile-wide Lake Nyos, about 200 miles north of the new republic's capital city of Yaoundé.

No one really knows the exact moment of the monster's birth. Most scientists, though, are reasonably sure that it was already there, on the lake bottom, in the terrible days of the 18th and early 19th centuries, when Arab traders – driving their slave caravans hard toward the sea – halted now and then along the riverbanks to unload the dead and dying for the crocodiles and vultures to feed upon. It was still growing in the early years of the 20th century, when

little steam trains, fueled by ebony and mahogany logs, labored inland at 10 miles per hour after stationmasters had used their rawhide whips to clear the tracks of natives. More recently, along the shores of Lake Nyos, grandfathers told grandchildren stories about the sultan of Ngaoundere, who commanded his 100-piece orchestra to play from dawn to dusk, and of the court executioner of Garoua, who carried dried parts of beheaded victims in a pouch around his neck.

But all that was long gone by the summer of 1986. The little valley communities around Lake Nyos, a crater lake whose slopes are prime agricultural land, were home to herdsmen and farmers. On the night of August 21 many of these hard-working people were already in bed or finishing up a late evening meal when there came, about 9.00pm, a distant rumble somewhere up by the lake that sounded like thunder. No one was surprised, for August is the rainiest month along the ridge of extinct volcanoes that runs along the Cameroonian-Nigerian border.

Then, in a flash, more than 1,700 people were dead. The agent of death? An enormous, invisible bubble of carbon dioxide. The monster had finally broken loose from the lake-bottom sediment and heavy water that had held it in check for centuries. Emerging from the blue surface of the lake like the most frightful genie in the *Arabian Nights*, the bubble killed everything and anything that breathed along the shoreline. Denser than air, the mile-wide gas cloud then flowed down into the adjacent valleys to carry out its deadly mission there. People, cattle, birds, and even ants were asphyxiated almost instantly.

Since there were so few survivors to report on the disaster, the officials in Cameroon were totally unaware of the tragedy. The first word they heard about it came through an unidentified government worker from the village of Wum. The man was traveling the 20 miles from his home to Lake Nyos on his motorcycle when he stopped to pick up a dead antelope on the road; it was a lucky find, for it would provide meat for the family he planned to visit. Shortly afterward, however, he felt dizzy, and then, to his horror, he began seeing dead human bodies sprawled everywhere along the route. Fearing what lay ahead, he turned and fled the way he had come, but his story was relayed to Bamenda, a provincial headquarters town, and a government official, Gideon Taka, was ordered to check it out. Taka, who reached the Lake Nyos area two days after the deadly cloud had struck, had trouble believing what he saw around him. "Most people were dead. They suffered burns, and those who were still surviving were coughing up blood," Taka later reported. "We saw a lot of corpses in the road; perhaps they thought they could survive by running away."

In the village of Cha, Francis Fang, a farmer, told an interviewer: "My wife dropped to the ground, vomiting blood. The children were burned and screaming. My wife was dead. I picked up my girls and started walking to the hospital. There were dead people everywhere on the road – so many I started stepping on them."

In another village, Nyos, only 4 of its 1,300 people survived. One young mother, Veronica Gmbie, lost five children, including her newest baby, whom she was holding in her arms. Jongi Zong, hurrying over from nearby Sumum, buried his brother and sister-in-law in one grave and their seven children in a second grave beside them. Fred Tenhorn, a Dutch priest, found an eerie scene, with all foliage green and healthy and corpses laid out underneath – "as if a neutron bomb had exploded," he said, killing everyone but leaving the landscape intact.

Even as various countries were channeling the first relief shipments of medicine and food to Cameroon, scientists were flying into the stricken country to study the results of the disaster firsthand. The French volcanologist François Leguern called the massacre at Lake Nyos "the worst volcanic gas disaster ever recorded." He believed that the eruption was the result of deep volcanic activity; but others, including the American experts from the US Office of Foreign Disaster Assistance, thought that an earthquake or landslide had freed the monstrous accumulation of gas from the lake's bottom.

But many of the sorrowing, frightened relatives and survivors were not interested in either theory. They had their own explanation for the exploding waters. Some remembered that three years earlier their tribal chief, on his death bed, had ordered that his finest, fattest cattle be driven off a cliff to drown in Lake Nyos, where the living spirits of the departed resided. But his family had ignored his wishes, and now the chief had had his revenge. Others blamed an angry Mammy Water, a spirit woman of the Cameroonian lakes and rivers, for the explosion.

We may never know what stirred the waters of Lake Nyos and turned the tranquil lake into the lake of death.

TASK

You have just read two articles, both of which were about rather strange but understandable disasters. The first probably has to do with the effect of the earth being struck by a very large meteorite; the second has to do with a natural occurrence.

1 Write two brief summaries, one of each passage, and explain in a brief paragraph at the end of each summary what explanation you think the evidence points to. Make sure in writing your summaries that you include only the facts which are relevant.

2 Choose one of the two events and imagine that you were present at the time and lived to tell the tale. Write your own version of what happened in about 300 words.

ANSWER

Neeru Kumar.   <u>Mysterious Fireball Blasts</u>
                                    <u>Siberia</u>

1   It took place on June 30, 1908, in a village full of Tungus people in central Siberia. The cause of the spectacular event, nobody knew. It all started with a blinding flash of light followed by a lit up sky.

Estimated to have been equal to about 30 million tonnes of T.N.T, everyone was baffled. Fearful sounds had filled the air along with strong tremors which had shaken the ground vigorously, and yet, Siberia wasn't the only country experiencing it. Places throughout the Northern Hemisphere were also hit by the blinding light.

Only until 22 years later did a British meteorologist recognise that the blast had acted as a vast solar reflector which illuminated the skies. Soon before this however, a Russian scientist named Leonid. A. Kulik had set out to explore the area hit by the "Fireball."

Only in 1927 with a local Tungus man did Kulik find any connection. A large area of forest land which was completely bare. This obviously proved that the explosion had taken place directly above this forest. Many theories have been put forward to explain this massive destruction. However, will the mystery ever be solved?

<u>Monster in Lake Nyos.</u>

Lake Nyos, the 600 ft deep lake in the North of Yaounde the capital city of Cameroon, was the cause of thousands of deaths. A huge bubble of gas which had planted itself on the lake bed had escaped on the night of August 21, 1986. The cause of the bubble was not familiar, however scientists believed that it was due to early days when Arab dealers used to dump the dead and dying.

There were hardly no witnesses to live and tell what had happened as the majority of the residents had died. Many people suffered burns however, some coughed up blood.

Many neighbouring countries had begun to send medical equipment and other relief aid. Not that much of it was needed, like in the village of Nyos only 4 of it's 1300 people survived. A young mother, Veronica Gmbie, Fred Tenhom a Dutch priest and "Jongi zong.

Explanation:-
"Fireball" - I think that was definitely something from outer space. Like a very large meteorite. It's hard to believe it was a U.F.O, because there would have been some traces of it.

"Monster." - I think this bubble of gas had something to do with the decomposition of people. I don't believe it was something spiritual.

Neeru Kumar.   Monster in Lake Nyos.

Veronica Gmbie.

2.   It was about 9·00 p.m in the
evening. I had just finished the washing
up after a late evening meal. It was
beginning to get late so I tucked all
my little children into bed. However
my new baby, Jonn wouldn't go to bed
until he had something to drink. So, I
went into our little kitchen to prepare
him a bottle of milk. That was when I
heard, it. There was a distant rumble of
thunder, or so I thought.

     Eventually Jonn went to sleep and so
I started mending some clothes before
I went to sleep. That was when everything went wrong. I heard screams and
shouts from my childrens bedroom. I
quickly dropped everything to go and
see what was wrong.

     I stepped into the dark room and
fumbled around for the latern. I soon
found it and that was the worst thing
I had ever seen. There was a whole
pool of blood on the floor. I stood
still for a moment and didn't know what
to do. All my children were now
covered in burns.

     I quickly picked up Jonn, my youngest
child and ran into the kitchen with
him. I turned on the cold water and
splashed it all over his burnt body.
However nothing would work. The burns
were just as bad and the screaming
was getting louder. After trying so hard,
I decided to just give up in the end.

     With tears pouring from my eyes, I ran
back into the children's room. All of them
were lying still on the floor. As still as
Jonn in my arms. I still didn't know
what had happened or how they had
died. However, whatever it was, it wasn't
going to get away with it.

Examiner's commentary   The summaries asked for here are not particularly easy and the
student has had to be very selective in taking the relevant facts from the passages. This is
at least in part because the passages are descriptive rather than tightly factual. The
candidate has, however, not wasted time and space with examples, and with speech and
speculation, but has done well in concentrating on the required facts. No particular guide
was given as to length other than the word "brief" and the student here has kept sensibly to
about a third of the length of the original.

   The student has also resisted the temptation to go off into the realms of speculation in the
concluding and additional paragraph to each summary. The conclusions which have been
drawn are sensible and plausible.

   The student's personal writing is very effective. The facts from "Monster in Lake Nyos"
have been well taken and the student has created a good atmosphere. There is some
selected specific reference especially to the mother with whom the student identifies.

STIMULUS
MATERIAL

Your Country

Geoffrey McKay is not the first person to have left the army because of racism. Now a race relations expert has been called in by a force which is hoping to recruit the best young people. Anna Pukas reports

eoffrey McKay adored the army. It had been his dream since childhood to join up, and, when he did, at 17, the army seemed to love him, too. Raised in the south London borough of Wandsworth, he was one of the brightest recruits of his intake at Catterick, winning awards for Best Gunner, Best At Drill and Best Signaller, and he was seconded to the careers office as a shining example of what the army could make of an ambitious young man. When he went off to join his regiment, the Queen's Royal Irish Hussars, in Fallingbostel, Germany, he was certain that he would be a soldier for life.

Less than two years later, the dream and Trooper McKay's military career were over. Things had begun to sour on his very first day in Germany, when his troop sergeant, Anthony Brownbill, called him "nigger" and asked him if he minded. McKay, whose mother is Sri Lankan and whose paternal grandfather came from the Virgin Islands, had never encountered overt racism before and said he did mind. Brownbill – who had already been reprimanded for similar behaviour with another soldier – accused him of being "another of those darkies with a chip on his shoulder" and warned him that he would have problems.

The sergeant was right. Over the next few months, the verbal abuse worsened, with fellow squaddies taking their lead from Brownbill. The name-calling turned into ostracism – McKay was not allowed to sit with anyone at mealtimes in the mess and took to eating alone in his room – and, eventually, to physical beatings. When he could stand no more, the young soldier went absent without leave twice, and then attempted suicide by swallowing insulin. In October 1992, 20 months after joining the army, McKay was given a medical discharge and, last month, he was awarded £8,000 compensation by an army board of inquiry. In what is believed to be an unprecedented distinction, £3,00 of the total was specifically awarded as punitive damages against the Ministry of Defence. The army, it seemed, was finally acknowledging that, far from being "colour-blind", some of its members were capable of racism.

That is the simplistic conclusion. The facts are that there would have been no inquiry if Geoffrey McKay had not had the support of the Commission for Racial Equality, and if the Prince of Wales had not demanded "necessary action" when McKay's family appealed to him for help. There would have been no investigation, because McKay's chief tormentor was his immediate commander, the troop sergeant, and he set the pattern for the others. Others further up the chain of command simply refused to accept that there even was a problem. One of them even insulted McKay's

parents when they wrote a letter of complaint. McKay was summoned, reprimanded for "snivelling", and told: "Tell your parents not to be so stupid." Even when it came to the hearing, senior soldiers expected to be believed above McKay, a mere lowly trooper. "But I'm an officer!" a major blurted out when McKay's barrister asked why his word should be given more credence.

Since the services are merito-cracies, how can discrimination exist? It is the reason given for never compiling the ethnic statistics of the men and women in the army, navy and airforce. "We look at anybody and will take anybody, regardless of background," says Commodore Ian Craig, the navy's head of recruitment. While that may be true, what none of the services has ever thoroughly addressed is how they treat non-white recruits once they are inside the services.

The first significant steps towards changing that will come later this year, with the first officially collected data on ethnicity in the armed forces. Questionnaires have been sent out to every serviceman and woman, while a code of practice on race relations has been circulated.

"This is all part of the armed forces' recognition that we live in a multicultural society, and of the need to emphasise that we are equal opportunities employers," says Brigadier Christopher Elliott, the director of army recruiting. "There are some excellent young people out there, from Asian and Afro-Caribbean families, who are highly educated and very motivated. We need a few trail-blazers to pull in the others, and they should have no doubts about racism being taken seriously. Anyone who condones or fails to stop racist behaviour would simply be ruining his own career."

These are all commendable sentiments, but, as with the police force before them, there is an unavoidable suspicion that the services have been pushed into embracing them. As with any society within a society, the forces have their own language and social mores. Behaviour which might be deemed extreme in other circles raises no eyebrows in the closed confines of a warship or garrison.

Letts
Q&A

Needs You

More pertinent is the fact that the armed forces are having to go on the offensive to recruit new members. Fewer young people are attracted to an organisation which, thanks to sweeping government cuts, appears to be shrinking daily; the navy is reducing its numbers from 65,000 10 years ago, to 53,000 by next year; the RAF will decline from more than 70,000 now to 52,500 by the end of the decade, and the army is down from 145,000 two years ago to 123,000 now. Despite this, the forces, of course, still need to attract young blood of the highest possible calibre. The army, for example, currently needs to receive 600 applications a week in order to sustain recruitment targets of 15,000 new soldiers a year, but is getting only 300 a week.

Besides, since the ethnic minority population is rising faster than the white population in Britain (it is set to double in the next forty years), any likelihood of "screening out" of non-whites, however subliminal, will soon be impossible. It will not even be a case of adopting quotas or positive discrimination (a strategy abhorrent to the armed forces) because it will be too late. In 1991, when Geoffrey McKay joined, he was one of 152 ethnic minority entrants – a tiny figure compared to the 12,847 whites who joined, but one which none the less shows that blacks and Asians not only crave a challenging career, but are also prepared to blaze trails.

Yet McKay was hounded out of the career he loved by the failure of his employers to take the necessary action – and, incidentally, fulfil a legal imperative – to keep him.

He was not the only one. In 1992, Private Anthony Evans, the son of a mixed-race mother, left the Royal Regiment of Wales after enduring seven years of abuse and isolation, after which he, too, was awarded compensation following a board of inquiry. Colleagues used to plunge him into baths and scrub him with yard brooms. He still suffers nightmares. "Meanwhile, the people who did the abusing are still in the army, as ignorant as ever," says his mother, Ann. "One has even been promoted."

The most prominent trail-blazer of all was Richard Stokes, the adopted black son of a white West Country family, who, in 1987, became the first black man in the elitist Brigade of Guards. In public relations terms, Stokes's recruitment to the Grenadier Guards was a gift from the gods. Only the year before, Prince Charles had expressed a particular wish to see a black face under a bearskin at the Changing of The Guard. After three years, Stokes, too, left, worn down by the daily cacophony of jungle noises and "Here comes the coon"; he was "overwhelmingly relieved that it's all over".

'if the generals and the colonels don't change their attitudes, all the smart marketing and codes of practice aren't worth the paper they're written on'

Following another case, where a corporal claimed that he was denied a transfer to the Household Cavalry because of his colour, the most visible military unit in the land is under investigation by the Commission for Racial Equality.

What will become of the monitoring statistics remains to be seen. The navy and RAF regard them as a means of "getting a handle on what our service actually looks like". Both Commodore Craig of the navy and Air Commodore Mike Butler, the RAF recruiting chief, deny that their service has a racism problem. Or, rather, as Craig says: "I am not aware of any racial harassment within the Royal Navy," which is not quite the same thing.

For the army's part, it has already approached the race relations expert Jerome Mack – a black former officer in the American air force – to school its recruiters and trainers. And therein lies the full extent of how little the armed forces as yet understand the insidious nature of racism.

"They believe the problem is merely about getting smarter at attracting recruits, but that is just a cosmetic approach," says Mack, who has been running residential courses in anti-racism for the British police forces for five years. "They trot out the same old excuses about blacks and Asians not having a military tradition, which puts the blame squarely back on blacks and Asians. The military here is just not sophisticated enough to acknowledge that there might be something wrong with it – or if it does, it believes it's a matter of procedure and not attitude. You know, get the marketing right and target the advertising better and it will all be okay. It is disingenuous, to say the least.

"I fully believe that the recruitment chiefs are sincere in what they want, but the changes in attitude are not made at their level. Their job is only input; it is the generals and the colonels of the regiments who take over once the new recruits are in, and if they don't change their attitudes, all the smart marketing and codes of practice aren't worth the paper they're written on.

"There is *no* pressure coming from within, and why? Because they say racism is down to a few bad apples, and a certain amount of bullying is the price you have to pay. Because they cannot see what they have to gain from it. They're wrong. What they do have to gain is a more professional army or navy or airforce, made up of the very best people they can get, and the ability to hold your head up among the nations and say we represent the best of our society. If that kudos does not motivate you, it will be a very long time before a Brit can reach the position of a Colin Powell in America."

Three years after his own motivation was crushed, former Trooper McKay can only agree. Now 23 and working for a jewellery company in London – Evans, meanwhile, is unemployed – McKay said last week: "It's all about education. It's ironic, because the armed forces are places where drumming something into people really works as a method of teaching; servicemen are used to it.

"The army always told me that as long as I performed I would be all right. Well, at no stage did anyone ever fault my work. I never asked for everyone to like me; I just wanted to be treated fairly and equally, like a professional. If the army had treated me in a professional manner, I would be still be there now."

Anne Pukas, *The Sunday Times* 31.7.94

Letts
Q&A

TASK

Read the passage carefully and then answer the following questions.

1 List the types of racial abuse which are referred to in the article.

2 The article refers to the armed forces as being "meritocracies". What do you understand by this term? Explain how this should mean less prejudice rather than more.

3 Explain the reasons which are clear in the passage why the armed forces themselves need to get rid of any prejudice.

4 EITHER Imagine you are McKay's parents and write the letter of complaint which they sent to his commanding officer.
OR Imagine that you are one of the black soldiers referred to in the article and write about your experience.

ANSWER

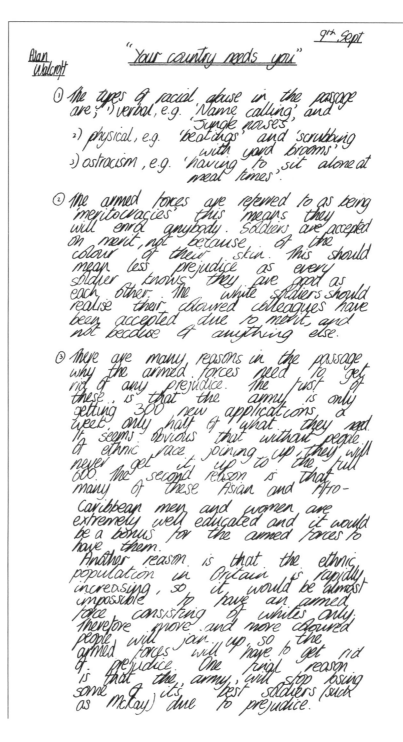

9th Sept

Alan Walcroft

"Your country needs you"

① The types of racial abuse in the passage are; 1) verbal, e.g. 'Name calling', and 'Jungle noises'.
2) physical, e.g. 'beatings' and 'scrubbing with yard brooms'.
3) ostracism, e.g. 'having to sit alone at meal times'.

② The armed forces are referred to as being 'meritocracies'. this means they will enrol anybody. Soldiers are accepted on merit, not because of the colour of their skin. This should mean less prejudice as every soldier knows they are good as each other. The white soldiers should realise their coloured colleagues have been accepted due to merit, and not because of anything else.

③ There are many reasons in the passage why the armed forces need to get rid of any prejudice. The first of these, is that the army is only getting 300 new applications a week, only half of what they need. It seems obvious that without people of ethnic race, joining up, they will never get it up to the full 600. The second reason is that many of these Asian and Afro-Caribbean men and women are extremely well educated and it would be a bonus for the armed forces to have them.
Another reason is that the ethnic population in Britain is rapidly increasing, so it would be almost impossible to have an armed force consisting of whites only; therefore more and more coloured people will join up, so the armed forces will have to get rid of prejudice. One final reason is that the army will stop losing some of it's best soldiers (such as McKay) due to prejudice.

4. Dear commanding Officer,
I am writing to voice my disgust at the way my son has been treated during his time in the army. On numerous occasions Geoffrey was subjected to, in my opinion, the worst kind of prejudice, racial prejudice. This as you may be surprised to here, as you seem to be totally ignorant is not just verbal, but also physical abuse. However my son said the worst thing was not being allowed to eat his dinner with the rest of the regiment.

I would like to know what is going to be done about this, and how you are going to discipline the culprits. I myself think they should be discharged from the army, although I doubt it you will go this far as you don't seem to recognise the problem as being serious.
At times the times the abuse was so intense, my son even attempted suicide, no person whatever race or colour should be forced to this, for other people's pleasure. One more than one occasion Geoffrey came running home to us in great distress, each time he implied he could no longer carry on being a part of the army.
I therefore hope you will do your best to get to the root of this problem and ensure that no more soldiers have to endure what Geoffrey did.

Yours Sincerely,
Mr and Mrs McKay
(Parents of Private McKay)

Examiner's commentary When a question asks you for a list then make sure that you write your answer in the form of a list. The student here has done this. Always make sure that you read instructions carefully.

The meaning of the word "meritocracy" can be deduced from the article and the candidate has answered this well. She may also have picked up the clue in the second sentence of the question.

For the third answer the candidate has headed straight for the most relevant part of the article when talking about recruitment. This is the key element to the answer.

The last question asks for an empathetic response and the student has done well here. She has been able to put herself in the place of the mother and there is a real feeling of personal care in the letter.

Perhaps one of the most important developments which has happened with GCSE English recently is that **speaking** and **listening** have become an integral part of the examination and count for 20% of your total possible marks.

Clearly this is important as speaking and listening are just as important, if not more important, as means of communicating, as writing is.

We have concentrated so far on written work using a variety of stimuli and requiring a variety of responses. Before we go on to the Exam Practice section let us think for a moment about speaking and listening.

Good practice at speaking and listening will help you gain marks for your coursework (speaking and listening are always assessed during the course), and it will also help you make progress in other parts of your English.

SPEAKING

There are two ways in which **oral work** takes place (often called **contexts**) i) **individual work;** ii) **work in pairs and in larger groups**. And there are a number of purposes to oral work: **presentation; planning; discussion**.

How can you improve at oral work? Let's look at each of the **contexts**:

❶ For **individual talks or presentations**, here is some advice: **plan** your main points in notes in order to **organise** your ideas, but not as a written essay – some talkers use index cards for their main points; the advantage of these is that you can keep them in order and discard them after each key point has been covered. Do not just talk, **communicate!** – use **eye contact**, change the **tone** and **pitch** of your voice, **pause** to give your listener a chance to take things in.

❷ For **pair or group planning and discussion**: concentrate on the task; be prepared to express new possible ideas; be supportive of others – certainly you can be critical, but never become destructive; be prepared to change your mind and entertain the views of others; try to be sensitive to other students you are working with – take up their points and ideas, draw them out if necessary, agree with them, encourage them (and remember to do all this with appropriate "body language" such as eye contact and smiles); **never just express a point of view without reasons – always back it up with evidence**; and do not hog the conversation – let others have their say!

DO I 'AVE TER SPEAK PROPER LIKE ME MUM AND DAD TOLD ME TER?

Styles of speech

You are not assessed on your accent, and do not try to use long words just for the sake of impressing others. But you are expected to speak in a register of standard English suitable for some situations in life. These would be more formal occasions, perhaps relating to work. You will obviously speak more informally amongst friends on less serious matters.

The most important thing to remember is that you must **communicate** and **express** your points well. It goes without saying that pupils who are interested in the world around them have more ideas to communicate!

GETTING THE IDEAS IN THE FIRST PLACE

As you go through your GCSE course, try to develop your views on important **issues in the news, or on controversial and moral topics**. You cannot possibly hope to do well in any speaking and listening tasks unless you have **ideas** of your own. Here are a few issues at random – what would your views be?: should the police be armed?; should workers have the right to use secondary picketing at strikes?; should there be a world ban on whaling?; what use is the citizens' charter?

KNOWLEDGE ABOUT SPOKEN LANGUAGE

In your exam you may be asked to comment on the way that spoken language works: this is a part of the National Curriculum in English known as **knowledge about language**. It is more likely that you would be asked to comment on examples of speech from a play or extracts of dialogue from scripts.

Here is a glossary of some useful terms to remember:

GLOSSARY

Standard English	English commonly spoken in a grammatical and readily understood fashion in formal contexts, e.g. the world of business, commerce, etc
Dialect	this is local variation of standard English
Accent	regional manner of pronunciation
Register	appropriate tone for speech (formal/informal/presentational/gossip/argument, etc)
Intonation	stress on different words, syllables, etc – used to emphasise key points – often termed the "punctuation of speech"
Mockery	speech used ironically, perhaps sarcastically, to create humour
Dialogue	two or more characters speaking with each other
Monologue	the opposite – a character speaking aloud to him or herself
Slang	alternative words used by groups of people, often all from the same area
Jargon	a sort of vocabulary known mostly to particular groups, e.g. of workers – "buzzwords" or an "in-language", maybe used exclusively
Tone	the mood of language (e.g. serious, mocking, sympathetic, etc.)

LISTENING

Sometimes it is easier to prepare yourself to speak and much more difficult to listen! In fact of all the things we do with language, listening may be the most difficult. How can you improve your listening skills?

The main approaches that you should practise are: **concentrate** as hard as you can on what is being said, and not so much on the way it is being said. As you are listening try not to be passive – this means that as well as taking in what you hear, you should actively be trying to think about what you hear. Other words for this skill are **analysing** or **interpreting**. Help the speaker through your own reactions and body language – remember that a good listener encourages a good speaker. Again, eye contact helps, as does an impression of concentration, perhaps nodding, smiling, agreeing. Above all do not become distracted and never put the speaker off by looking away or yawning!

This last section of the book is designed to give you as many chances as possible to practise your skills. For English practice may not always make perfect but it does give you a chance to think and improve and is probably the best way there is to revise.

This section is split into two parts, the first part has a selection of tasks, many of which are taken from GCSE exam papers, and the second part contains Examiner's tips which advise you on how to approach the various tasks.

Each task has a brief introduction, followed by some stimulus material and then the task itself. Please have a go at the tasks first and then read the tips to see if your approach is what was expected. If you are way out of line with what was expected you might then choose to have another go. Practise hard and good luck with your examination!

TASK 1

In this first example we have taken a couple of extracts from a booklet of material which was issued to candidates in advance of the examination. There were in fact twenty-one different pieces in the booklet.

STIMULUS MATERIAL

Rose Gamble recalls her childhood in Chelsea during the 1920s.

At playtime I was given my paper bag and ventured alone into the playground. After the orderly classrooms, the playground was bedlam. I watched what the other kids were doing. Most of them played chasing, pushing each other clean off their feet. Others jumped up and down with a continuous shout into each other's faces. Long strings of small boys chunted behind each other, playing trains, winding their way through the crowds. Some just squatted down against the walls, their faces pinched, their hands drawn up into their sleeves. I wandered over to the shed, which was for shelter, for we were sent out to play whatever the weather. It was simply a roof built over a corner where two of the playground walls joined, with the open side supported by brick columns. One of the walls had been painted with dark green paint, and along the bottom ran a wooden bench about eighteen inches high. The bench was the scene of the simplest and most excitingly savage game I had ever seen. A boy, or a girl, leapt on the bench, and leaned hard against the wall with braced legs. It was the object of one or a group of several other kids to nudge, push, shove or pull him off, and for the quickest to hop up and take his place. Four or five of these games were going on at the same time all along the bench. Kids shot up and disappeared like skittles. They landed on the bench skilfully shoving a knee behind the defender in one movement and levered him off, giving him a wild push to send him on his way sprawling on the asphalt. Some were bodily yanked by the arms and twisted to the ground with jersey sleeves stretching a foot over their hands. One lot all fell down as two girls came hurtling together off the bench on top of them, screeching with grazed knees and bashed fingers. Noses ran, boots, socks and trousers were scuffed with grey dust, bloomer legs trailed over knees and the noise reached fever pitch as the games got faster and faster. The bell rang, and just as in the morning everyone stood still as stone, panting and grinning, red-faced and filthy. The din of children's voices echoed for a moment round the shed and then in the stillness there was the faint clap of a pigeon's wing. At the second bell I stole into my line still carrying my unopened paper bag. I hadn't remembered to go to the lav either.

From a short story *Homecoming* by William McIlvanney.

'Going home,' she said.

'Graithnock,' she said.

'London,' she said.

'Frances Ritchie,' she said.

She treated his questions like spaces in an official form, impersonally, never digressing into humanising irrelevance. I am a stranger on a train, she was saying. She asked him nothing in return.

But the man was persistent. He had come on at Dumfries, entering a coach clogged with the boredom of several hours' travel, the unfinished crosswords, the empty whisky miniatures interred in their plastic cups, the crumpled beer cans rattling minutely to the motion of the train. Picking his way among the preoccupied stares and the occasionally stretched legs, he had sat down opposite Fran. The seats had only just been vacated by a mother and a small girl who had made Fran wonder if her own desire for children was as deep as she told herself it was.

His persistence wasn't offensive. It had none of the I-secretly-know-what-you-want-and-need machismo which Fran had learned to recognise from a distance like a waving flag and which caused her to shoot on sight. his persistence was gentle, slightly vulnerable, as if he had decided – for no reason that she could understand – that he wanted to please her. Although it was a smoker, he asked if she minded him smoking.

'Just thought I'd check,' he said. 'The way it's going these days, they'll be issuing a leper's bell with every packet.'

Her smile disappeared like a mistake being erased.

'So what took you from Graithnock to London'

She looked out of the window. Would she have known that countryside was Scotland if the stations they passed through hadn't told her?

'The train,' she said. 'The 12.10 I think it was.'

The sharpness of her remark made her glance toward his silence. He was smiling.

'You gave some extra information there,' he said. 'Does that mean you're softening towards me?'

'I wouldn't bet on it,' she said.

But she was laughing. She noticed he had a smile as open as a blank cheque. In spite of herself, she felt the moment put down roots and blossom into one of those sudden intimacies between strangers. He discovered that she was a journalist. He claimed to have seen her byline. ('That's what you call it? Isn't it? A byline?') He convinced her by getting the newspaper right. He was a Further Education lecturer in English at Jordanhill College in Glasgow. He had been on a visit to students in Dumfries.

'I prefer taking the train when I can,' he said. 'You go by car, it's just a chore, isn't it? This way, you can turn it into a carnival. Watch. Just answer one question, that's all we need. What do you drink?'

He came back from the buffet with two gins and two cans of tonic for her, two whiskies and a plastic cupful of water for himself. They made a party between them. As with all good parties, the conversation went into overdrive.

'The new Glasgow?' he said. 'What difference is it making to the people in the housing-schemes? How many investors invest for the good of others? That kind of investment's the Trojan Horse, isn't it? Oh, look, these nice punters are giving us a prezzy. Let's bring it into the city. Then, when it's dark, its belly opens and they all come out to loot and pillage.'

'I think maybe *Manhattan*,' she said. 'But it's not exactly an easy choice. I still love *Play it again, Sam*, that scene where the hairdrier almost blows him away. I just think he's great. Who was it said that? Bette Midler? "You want to take him home and burp him." '

'Maybe I just haven't found the man,' she said. 'You volunteering? I'm involved at the moment, actually, But I don't think marriage is exactly imminent.'

'It's interesting enough,' she said. 'But you go to a lot of places without really seeing them. Because you're there for one purpose. It can be like travelling in a tunnel.'

'Oh, that was the worst time,' he said. 'Don't worry about it. Divorce? I can see what Dr Crippen was getting at. I'm not saying I agree with him. But murder must be a lot less hassle.'

Before the buffet closed ('Haven't we been lucky?' he said. 'They usually shut it about Carlisle, but the fella in the buffet's drunk.'), she went and fetched them two more drinks. By the time they were drawing into Graithnock she had his telephone number (but he didn't have hers) and Fran was about to say goodbye to Tom.

Departure heightened their sense of closeness. He was helping her with her case and threatening to come with her since he felt it only right, considering how far they were along the road to marriage, that he should meet her parents. Just before he opened the door for her, he kissed her on the cheek.

Then she was on the platform with her case beside her and he was leaning out, waving with mock drama, and she felt slightly dazed with alcohol and elation, as if she were taking part in a scene from a film in which she might be the heroine and didn't know what would happen next, and then she turned and saw her parents.

They were standing thirty yards away, waiting for her to notice them. They would be doing that – not for them the spontaneity of running towards her. Victor and Agnes Ritchie, informal as a letterhead. They stood slightly apart, her father with his clipped, grey military moustache, a general in the army of the genteel, her mother with that expression some unknown experience had pickled on her face countless years ago. Fran wondered again how they had acquired their ability to turn joy into a dead thing at a touch and how they had managed to pass the gift on to her. Years of hopelessness they had taught her resurfaced in her at once. She suspected the value of the pleasure she had just had.

Her life in miniature, she thought, this journey. A promise something in her wouldn't allow her to fulfil. She didn't think she would be phoning him. She hoped she would but, standing there, she would have bet against it. She felt her faith in life and living evaporate. Her parents had taught her well. Maybe home is simply where you can't get away from, she thought.

As she lifted her case and walked towards them, she fingered the return ticket in the pocket of her jacket, wondering how far she would have to go finally to get away from here.

TASK Choose one of the characters. Imagine you have to interview him or her about the conflict he or she has experienced. Write your interview.

You may use question and answer form if you wish. Name the character you interview.

SEG 1994

Here you are given quite a dense passage to read. There is a lot of information and what you are going to be asked to do is to summarise the information. The article is about crime.

Out of the mouths of babes

In a new survey young people describe their experiences of crime and suggest possible causes and solutions.

Young people are just as worried by their parents by the cases reported in the media and by crime which they suffer themselves, according to a new survey by criminologists. In fact, youngsters could be said to have more reason to fear violent crime because they are its most common victims.

A team of researchers carried out the survey on two large estates near Birmingham. They questioned 307 youngsters who were aged between thirteen and seventeen about crime, its causes and possible solutions.

Their findings contradict the view of some public figures that juvenile crime is increasing. The findings show that very few teenagers are involved in stealing cars, burglary, robbery and assaults.

The 148 boys and 159 girls questioned were from families with high levels of unemployment. A high percentage had single parents and most were still at school.

Two out of every five boys and girls had played truant from school, a quarter regularly smoked and about seven out of ten had drunk alcohol. Roughly a fifth said they had taken money from home and a smaller percentage had shoplifted.

33 per cent of the boys, and 26 per cent of the girls, said they had hit and injured somebody in a public place. Only one per cent had broken into a house or shop. Three per cent, girls as well as boys, had taken a vehicle and driven it away. Seven per cent had used a weapon in a fight, but twice as many carried weapons for protection.

But what came through most strongly was the large number of youngsters who had also been the victims of crime or the threat of crime. Fifteen per cent had been stopped by

male drivers they did not know and asked to get into their cars. Similar numbers had been followed by a stranger in a car or on foot. A fifth said they had been assaulted in the street.

When asked why youngsters they knew committed crimes, 79 per cent cited boredom and 58 per cent said the offenders had no sense of right and wrong. A lack of leisure facilities was blamed by half and 44 per cent blamed parental neglect.

More police officers on foot patrol was the most popular solution for reducing juvenile crime, and was suggested by nearly seven out of ten. 65 per cent said there should be more discipline and supervision by parents.

In fact, the majority of those surveyed revealed the presence of caring parents. Seven out of ten were taken out by parents and 61 per cent said their parents wanted to know where they were and what they were doing at all times. 85 per cent said they could talk to their mother or father about anything that troubled them.

Three-quarters had never been hit by either parent but were shouted at or threatened for wrongdoing, whereas sixteen per cent were hit sometimes or often. 69 per cent said their parents explained to them why certain things were wrong.

The findings still need proper analysis and will not be published for another year. But we can already see that there is agreement among young people and adults about strategies for preventing crime and why young people offend.

Are our kids out of control? The answer is no, but there is a substantial minority of children who are neglected. You can deduce from that that those children are more likely to get involved in crime if there is nobody checking up on them.

In the past, eighteen-to-twenty-one-year-old working-class kids got jobs and got married. The best antidote to crime is a steady job and a steady relationship.

(Adapted from the Guardian, March 1993)

TASK

Summarise what the survey has to say about:

● the background of the young people interviewed,

● the offences they admitted to,

● the reasons they gave for juvenile crimes,

● their suggestions for solving the problem of juvenile crimes,

● their relationship with their parents.

MEG 1994

TASK 3

Quite often you might be asked simply to write imaginatively as was the case in this next example. Reproduced below is the task and the stimulus exactly as it appeared on the examination paper. In some ways you might argue that you are given very little to go on...

STIMULUS MATERIAL

This passage is adapted from the opening chapter of *Bleak House* by Charles Dickens.

London ... November weather. As much mud in the streets, as if the waters had but newly retired from the face of the earth ... Smoke lowering down from chimney-pots, making a soft black drizzle with flakes of soot in it as big as full-grown snowflakes – gone into mourning, one might imagine, for the death of the sun. Dogs, undistinguishable in mire. Horses, scarcely better; splashed to their very blinkers. Foot passengers, jostling one another's umbrellas, in a general infection of ill-temper, and losing their foot-hold at street corners, where tens of thousands of other foot passengers have been slipping and sliding since the day broke (if this day ever broke), adding new deposits to the crust upon crust of mud ...

Fog everywhere. Fog up the river, where it flows among green aits and meadows; fog down the river, where it rolls defiled among the tiers of shipping ... Fog on the Essex marshes, fog on the Kentish heights. Fog creeping into the cabooses of collier-brigs; fog lying out on the yards, and hovering in the rigging of great ships; fog drooping on the gunwales of barges and small boats. Fog in the eyes and throats of ancient Greenwich pensioners, wheezing by the firesides of their wards; fog in the stem and bowl of the afternoon pipe of the wrathful skipper, down in his close cabin; fog cruelly pinching the toes and fingers of his shivering little 'prentice boy on deck. Chance people on the bridges peeping over the parapets into a nether sky of fog, with fog all around them, as if they were up in a balloon, and hanging in the misty clouds.

TASK

Write the opening section of a novel. Link the setting to the place, the weather and the action.

NEAB 1994

Earlier in this book we used an example of a fairly short answer comprehension test and this is what we have here. What is printed below is one section of the examination paper. We have reproduced it almost exactly as it appeared because the questions take you systematically through the story referring to particular lines.

TASK 4

Read carefully the short story below. Then answer **all** the questions which follow.

STIMULUS MATERIAL

Some Day My Prince Will Come

It's Saturday. Working on the House Day. Every weekend Martin works on the house. Weekends of fogs of dust and muffled curses from the closed door behind which he toils… of tripping over the plumbing pipes and searching for one small sandal in the rubble and keeping out of Daddy's way.

5   Anyway, that Saturday I got up and fed the children and peeled the plasticine from Martin's hammer before he saw it. Really, compared to the rest of the week, weekends were such a strain. I pulled a nail out of Tilly's shoe and she made such a fuss that I tried to shut her up by telling her a story. And Adam fell down and shrieked so badly that Martin heard him over the electric sander.

After lunch Martin went out. He had all these errands to do on Saturdays, like getting his hair
10 cut and things mended that I had forgotten to do during the week or that I had been far too busy to fetch. He can't understand that I'm busy, when there's nothing to show for it. No floors relaid, nothing like that. And he has to go to all these proper little shops with old men in overalls who take hours; he refuses to go to the big help-yourself places because he says they're soulless.

It was two thirty and raining outside. The afternoon stretched ahead; Adam was staggering
15 around, scattering wood shavings. Then I looked in the paper and saw that "Snow White" was on. So I wrote a note to Martin and heaved out the double buggy.

"Does Snow White wear a beautiful pink dress?" Tilly asked. She's obsessed with pink.

"Can't remember," I said. "I was your age when I saw it. I loved it more than any other film I've ever seen."
20   "Snow White gets deaded," said Adam.

"She doesn't!" I cried. "She's only asleep. She wakes when the Prince comes along and kisses her."

When did Martin last kiss me? Properly. Or when, indeed, did I last kiss him?

We arrived at the cinema. A peeling brick cliff, its neon lights glaring over the grey street. How
25 could such buildings house such impossible dreams?

Inside I saw *him* for the first time in ten years. I saw him straight away. I had sat next to him in fifty cinema seats. Him beside me, his arm lying along the back of the seat. But now his arms were flung each side of his children.

The cinema darkened. Snow White was washing the steps, scrubbing and singing. I thought:
30 forgot the Daz and now I've missed the shops.

"When's the Prince coming?" hissed Tilly. "Will he come on his horse?"

"Of course."

He'd had a motorbike. I'd sat behind him, gripping him with my arms, my face pressed against the leather. My parents were terrified that I would marry him. But I didn't, did I? All I'd heard
35 was that he was married and had two children. She was called Joyce. With a name like that she must be overweight.

The Dark Queen was up on the screen with her bitter, beautiful face. A hand gripped mine.

"She's horrid," said Tilly.

"She's jealous," I whispered.
40   The hand squeezed. "She's turning into a witch."

"I don't like her," I said.

Tilly said in her posh voice, "It's because she's got ugly thoughts." I had a sudden desire to grip my growing wayward girl and protect her from what lay ahead. But she disliked shows of emotion.

45 Snow White let in the witch. As she took the apple, the audience sat absolutely still. All those children – not a sweet paper rustled. Nothing.

When she bit the apple, Tilly hid her face.

"It's all right," I said desperately. "I told you, the Prince will come."

He came of course, as you knew he would. The Prince knelt down to kiss Snow White. And

50 then she was in his arms and he was lifting her onto his horse. Not a motorbike – a stallion of pure white, and the sun cast long shadows between the trees as they rode off, and ahead lay the castle, radiant.

"Where's your hanky?' I muttered.

I took her handkerchief and blew my nose. The lights came on.

55 "Don't be soppy," said Tilly. "It's only a story."

Twenty minutes later I was walking up our street. The eye of the bedroom window looked at me and said: Shouldn't have gone, should you?

The car was outside and the lights were on. Martin must be home. The rain stopped but I wiped my face on my sleeve. He would just think my face was wet from the rain. If, that is, he

60 noticed anything about me.

I went into the house. There was a forest of planks in the hall. He had been to the timber merchant. Martin didn't come out of the kitchen. No buzzing drill. I hesitated. Could he read my thoughts?

Then I thought: He's made me a surprise.

65 I stood still and let the realization fill me, through my limbs, like warm liquid.

Martin had made the supper. Hopelessly, because he can't cook. But he had cleared the table and bought a bottle of wine and lots of expensive things from the delicatessen. He realized how I'd been feeling lately.

I opened the door. But this wasn't a story. Life is not that neat, is it? No fairy tale.

70 There sat Martin, with a can of beer in front of him and the lunch plates still piled in the sink. Packets were heaped on the table; not exotic cheeses but boxes of screws and nails.

He looked up. "Didn't hear you come in."

"Exhausted?" I asked.

He nodded. Fiction is shapely. A story billows out like a sheet, then comes the final knot. The

75 End. Against the pink sky stands a castle, lit from within. The End.

A silence as he poured the beer into his glass. He said, "The end is in sight. I think I can finally say I've finished this bloody kitchen."

(Adapted from "Some Day My Prince Will Come" by Deborah Moggach)

TASK

Look again at lines 1–16

1 What are your first impressions of the writer and the life she leads? Give reasons for your opinions. (10)

Look again at lines 17–55

2 The writer comes out of the cinema in tears. What happens to make her so upset? Why do you think she reacts as she does? (10)

Look again at lines 56–77

3 What happens after the writer leaves the cinema? What do you think about this as an ending to the story? (10)

To answer the next question you will need to think about the story as a whole.

4 What do you think about the relationship between the writer and her husband, Martin? Give reasons for your opinions. (10)

WJEC 1994

This 1994 paper gave another chance to do some personal writing. First of all there is a picture and then there are three associated possible tasks. In this case each of the tasks requires a different style of writing. The first is a particularly personal piece of writing; the second is a piece of discursive writing where you are asked to express an opinion; the third is imaginative. You might like to practise by doing all three tasks and then deciding which task you felt you coped best with and was most satisfying.

TASK 5

STIMULUS MATERIAL

FIRST   **Look at the picture of a young person fishing.**
NEXT   Think of outdoor sports, hobbies and activities.

TASK

| *WHAT YOU HAVE TO WRITE* |

1 **Write about** a particularly memorable day when you took part in an outdoor activity either on your own **or** with a group.

    OR

2 "Hunting, shooting and fishing"
    Discuss the view that such activities are cruel.

    OR

3 **Write a short story** in which a river plays an important part.

SEB 1994

TASK 6

The next example that we are taking from a 1994 examination paper involves quite a substantial amount of reading and we suggest that you tackle one question which needs careful reading and analysis to complete it successfully.

STIMULUS MATERIAL

When the writer was a boy, he lived in the countryside with his father on the island of Trinidad in the West Indies. After his father's death, he moved with his mother to Port-of-Spain, the island's capital city.

I had always considered this woman, my mother, as the enemy. She was sure to misunderstand anything I did, and the time came when I thought she not only misunderstood me, but quite definitely disapproved of me. I was an only child, but for her I was one too many.

She hated my father, and even after he died she continued to hate him.

She would say, 'Go ahead and do what you are doing. You are your father's child, you hear, not mine.'

My mother had decided to leave my father, and she wanted to take me to her mother. I refused to go.

My father was ill, and in bed. Besides, he had promised that if I stayed with him I was to have a whole box of crayons.

I chose the crayons and my father.

In fact, my mother moved us to Port-of-Spain where I saw what the normal relationship was between the beater and the beaten – when I saw this I was grateful.

My mother made a great thing at first about keeping me in my place and knocking out all the nonsense my father had taught me. I don't know why she didn't try harder, but the fact is that she soon lost interest in me, and she let me run about the street, only rushing down to beat me from time to time.

Occasionally, though, she would take the old firm line.

One day, she kept me home. She said, 'No school for you today. I am sick of tying your shoelaces for you. Today you will have to learn that!'

I didn't think she was being fair. After all, in the country none of us wore shoes and I wasn't used to them.

That day she beat me and beat me and made me tie knot after knot and in the end I still couldn't tie my shoelaces.

Still there were surprising glimpses of kindness.

There was the time, for instance, when I was cleaning some tumblers for her one Saturday morning. I dropped a tumbler and it broke. Before I could do anything about it my mother saw what had happened.

She said, 'How did you break it?'

I said, 'It just slipped off. It was smooth smooth.'

She said, 'A lot of nonsense drinking from glass. They break so easy.'

And that was all. I got worried about my mother's health.

She was never worried about mine.

She thought that there was no illness in the world a stiff dose of hot Epsom Salts couldn't cure.

And if there was something she couldn't understand, she sent me to the Health Office in Tragerete Road. That was an awful place. You waited and waited before you went in to see the doctor.

My mother considered the Health Office a good place for me to go to. I would go there at eight in the morning and return any time after two in the afternoon. It kept me out of mischief, and it only cost twenty-four cents a year.

But you mustn't get the impression that I was a saint all the time. I wasn't. I used to have odd fits where I just couldn't take an order from anybody, particularly my mother. I used to feel that I would dishonour myself for life if I took anybody's orders. And life is a funny thing, really. I sometimes got these fits just when my mother was anxious to be nice to me.

I wrote an essay for my schoolmaster on the subject, 'A Day at the Seaside'. I don't think any schoolmaster ever got an essay like that. I talked about how I was nearly drowned and how calmly I was facing death, with my mind absolutely calm, thinking, 'Well, boy, this is the end.' The teacher was so pleased he gave me ten marks out of twelve.

He said, 'You are a genius.'

When I went home and told my mother, 'That essay I wrote today, I got ten out of twelve for it.'

My mother said, 'How do you lie so in front of my face? You want me to give you a slap to turn your face?'

In the end I convinced her.

She melted at once. She sat down in the hammock and said, 'Come and sit down by me, son.'

Just then the crazy fit came on me.

I got very angry for no reason at all and I said, 'No, I – not going to sit by you.'

She laughed and coaxed.

And the angrier she made me.

Slowly the friendliness died away. It had become a struggle between two wills. I was prepared to drown rather than dishonour myself by obeying.

'I told you to come and sit here.'

'I am not sitting down.'

'Take off your belt.'

I took it off and gave it to her. She belted me soundly, and my nose bled, but still I didn't sit in the hammock.

At times like this I used to cry, without meaning it, 'If my father was here you wouldn't be behaving like this.'

So she remained the enemy. She was someone from whom I was going to escape as soon as I grew big enough. That was, in fact, the main lure of adulthood.

I was travelling by bus, one of the green buses of Sam's Super Service, from Port-of-Spain to Petit Valley.

My head felt as though it would split, but when I tried to shout out I found I couldn't open my mouth. I tried again, but all I heard, more distinctly now, was the constant chattering.

Water was pouring down my face.

I was flat out under a tap and there were faces above me looking down.

Someone said, 'How you feeling?'

I said, trying to laugh, 'I feel all right.'

A voice asked, 'You have any pains?'

I shook my head.

But suddenly, my whole body began to ache. I tried to move my hand and it hurt.

I said, 'I think I've broken my hand.'

But I could stand, and they made me walk into the house.

My mother came and I could see her glassy and wet with tears.

Somebody, I cannot remember who, said, 'Boy, you had your mother really worried.'

I looked at her tears, and I felt I was going to cry too. I had discovered that she could be worried and anxious for me.

Write down separately the advice you would give the mother, and the advice you would give to the boy, to help them to improve their relationship.

ULEAC 1994

TASK

TASK 7 You are sometimes given quite a lot of stimulus material and the first thing to do is to read it carefully. When the examiners set a paper they consider the length of the stimulus material and make allowances for the time that you will take to read it. So do not worry if you spend some time reading and thinking – you must do this before you start writing.

This stimulus material and the questions which follow are based on the idea of "WORKING AWAY". In the past few years cheaper air travel and fewer passport controls or restrictions on where people can go have encouraged many young people to travel abroad. More recently, the abolition of many employment requirements within the European Community has made it possible to find work in other countries as well.

Printed below you will find a leaflet about working abroad. You will also find details of four possible jobs. Read this material carefully and make use of it to answer the questions which follow.

STIMULUS MATERIAL

WANTING TO WORK AWAY THIS SUMMER?

FOLLOW THESE DOs AND DON'Ts FOR SUCCESS AND SAFETY

Every year thousands of young people find jobs in other parts of Europe and now, with the opening of Eastern European countries to foreigners, there are more opportunities than ever to live in other communities and to see different places.

DO ✓

Find a job before you set off.

Make sure your terms of employment are clearly set out in writing.

Look around and find work which suits your personality and abilities.

Buy a return ticket so that if things go wrong you can leave.

Apply for work through student organisations or well-known agencies.

Check whether you need a permit or visa of any kind before you set off.

Apply for several jobs and compare what they can offer you.

DON'T ✗

Take the first job you see.

Break your agreements. It makes it more difficult for others next time.

Expect jobs to be easy. You're cheap, casual labour and will be made to work hard.

Leave arrangements to the last minute.

Take work offers from people at airports and railway stations.

Ignore local employment laws and regulations.

To find out more about job opportunities in Europe and America look in student magazines or contact your nearest agency.

A

PARENTS PLUS – FRANCE
10 Orwell Road, Felixstowe,
Suffolk IP7 2RQ
(Tel: 0394 46201)

AU PAIRS, and **NANNIES** can be placed by this organisation with families all over France. Monthly salaries of up to £350. Board and accommodation is provided by the family. Minimum age 18 years. Minimum length of stay usually 6–12 months, but during the summer, from June until September, there are vacancies for 3 months and a few for 1–2 months' stays, applications for which should be made between April and June. Write to the Organiser at the above address giving full details of availability.

B

HOTEL "STROMBOLI": Corso Mameli No. 78, 30850 Verbania Intra (Novara), Italy

WAITING STAFF. £63 per month. To work from 09.30–15.00 and 18.30–21.00 (including meal breaks) 6 days per week. Free board and accommodation provided. Period of work from July 1st–September 30th: minimum period of work 1 month, which must not end between August 1st and 20th.

Applications to Signora Carmine Gianna at the above address

C

MARQUEE HOLIDAYS LIMITED

**Courier Department
189 Bath Road
Basingstoke
Hants
☎ 0256 92220**

RESIDENTIAL COURIERS (pre university students and undergraduates) to work on camp sites. Wages around £100 per week. Duties are varied but in short they involve welcoming and looking after customers, helping with any problems that may arise and maintaining tents and equipment. Accommodation and cooking facilities provided in large frame tents. Candidates are required to be proficient in French or Italian: experience in working with people and camping is desirable. Must be fit, responsible and self-reliant. Periods of work either from the end of April to mid-July or early July to the end of September.

☛ *Write to Mr G Small at the above address*

D

CENTRO AMUNO DI STUDI PREISTORICI: 25044 Capo di Ponte, Brescia, Italy

VOLUNTEERS (*5 positions*) to work for an archaeological institute specialising in the study of prehistoric rock art. The work involves editing, translating and working in the laboratory and library. Applicants should have an interest in archaeology, anthropology and/or art history, and have a good command of at least two languages – English, Italian, French, Spanish or German. Free accommodation and one meal per day provided. 5 days per week for a minimum of 2 months; dates of work by arrangement.

Applications to Erica Simoes de Abreu at the above address.

TASK

1   Read the notes below which describe the qualifications and interests of five young people. Giving your reasons, state which of the **four jobs described on the insert** each of them **could** apply for. Briefly say which job you think they would be most suited for. **The first one is done for you to show how to set out your answer.**

> **JASON:** Seventeen years old, GCSE grade B French, studying Biology, History and Art at College. Available from 1st July–15th August. Has to be home for sister's wedding on August 17th. Likes working with groups of people.
>
> *Because Jason is only seventeen he cannot work for Parents Plus and his availability means he cannot do jobs B or C either. He would be suited to job D because of his interest in art and history plus the fact that he has a good grade in French.*

SHARON: Eighteen years old, has just taken A level French, available until end of September when she starts a secretarial course at college. Likes travel and has been on German and French exchanges from school. Wants to be independent and 'her own boss'.

LLOYD: Eighteen years old, GCSE French Grade D, available from June to end of September. Wants to make money by working for two months and then to travel round.

SUSIE: Seventeen years old, having a year off before going to Cardiff University to study History. Has had work experience previously with a market research organisation. Has studied French and German.

JING: Eighteen years old, speaks English, some Spanish and Chinese. Available from June. She hasn't travelled in Europe before.

2   Choose **one** of the advertised posts and compose your own letter of application. This is a formal letter and should be set out appropriately with your address and the name and address of the person you are writing to included.

In your letter make sure that you describe yourself, say why the position interests you, when you are available and why you think you are suitable for it.

To help you do this, you can invent, and add, details about one extra language you can speak, one skill that you have qualifications in (like typing, cooking or sport) and one piece of relevant experience that will support your application.

3 Write an article for a magazine for young people about summer jobs in Europe for school-leavers and students. The article should be around 350 words long with a lively title and opening paragraph and helpful sub-headings. It will need to mention the kinds of work which are available, the variations in wages and conditions, and the precautions which people should take in applying for work and accepting job offers.

4 Read this letter sent to a travel magazine and published as 'Problem of the Week'. Write your reply, dealing with the points Dorothy Rood makes, as if you worked for the magazine.

Dear Travel Update,

I'm worried about my daughter, Rachel. She only left school last summer and after a year at college she wants to go off and work somewhere in Germany with one of her friends. She thinks they can work at a holiday camp or something like that.

She wants me to help her with her passport and to sign some papers to say she's eighteen – she will be in three months' time anyway – and I don't know whether I should.

I've heard about young kids just disappearing when they go abroad and being made to carry drugs and things by people they meet and I know Rachel is easily led at times.

I'd be happier with someone keeping an eye on her but I know she's growing up and has to be independent as well. What can I do?

Yours sincerely,

Dorothy Rood

MEG 1994

TASK 8 In this next example you will see a number of pieces of stimulus material which are all on the theme of "Bullying". You will notice that the sources of the material are very different: the first piece is from literature; the second is from a newspaper; the third is from a leaflet which is giving advice.

They are, all together, very good examples of what is meant by "writing in different styles and for different audiences". They all look different on the page and use different vocabulary.

When you get on to the questions it is very important to note that you are expected to use all the material and, quite clearly, to gain all the credit you want, it is essential that you do just that.

STIMULUS MATERIAL

Read the following extracts carefully; then answer questions 1 and 2.

In the story, set in India (Extract A), Farrukh Dhondy tells an incident from his schooldays. After the newspaper article about bullying (Extract B), there is some advice published by the organisation 'Kidscape' about how to deal with a bully (Extract C).

Extract A

Terry Soakum was a boarder. He was a white boy and came to our class for the first time, ushered by an Anglo-Indian matron, in tears. His arrival caused a quickly quelled stir in the class. There was one other white boy at the school and there had been a third.

We gathered round the new arrival at break time. He sobbed silently and he was shown how to lock his desk and make up his time-table. Through his sobs and his wet eyes which stared at one spot, he made it known that he was from Australia, from Perth. He had cried all the way on the plane. We never thought of asking him how he'd landed up in Poona.

He was a curiosity to the rest of the school and crowds gathered to see him, as though a strange animal had been imported to the old zoo. He wasn't wearing school uniform and continued for the next few days in his blue velvet shorts and frilled silk shirt. He carried a painted boomerang with him.

On the fourth day that Soakum was there he was summoned to the presence of our gang. Its leader was Farokh Habibulla, commonly known as Haby. He was the only boy who was seventeen and was growing a moustache amongst the day scholars. The rest of us were fourteen and fifteen. He was a veteran. He had spent three years in the tenth standard because he hadn't passed his exams. He was a weight-lifter. His muscles bulged out of rolled-up sleeves. He gave demonstrations of his strength by shaking the trunks of well-established trees and he always managed to speak, to teachers and to the rest of us, in a growl which seemed to come from way down in his guts.

'Send for the Australian,' he said.

A couple of the gang went to seek out the Soakum circus, the jeering bunch of third and fourth standard tykes who followed Soakum around wherever he went. In a few minutes, Soakum was brought to us.

'I hope you like India,' Farokh Habibulla said.

'I don't like the boys, they're not nice boys. In Australia…'

'In Australia people smell like sheep,' Haby said.

'Tell him please, to let go of my arm. It hurts,' Soakum shrieked. The gathering laughed.

Haby gave a vague signal with his eyebrows and Terry Soakum was released.

'All right, now give me that crooked stick.'

'It's a boomerang.'

'How much does it cost?'

'You can't buy it in rupees. It costs pounds, shillings and pence.'

'That's all right then. If I can't buy it I'll take it.'

Haby stretched his hand out. Soakum quickly held the boomerang behind his back. Haby wriggled his fingers. Two boys detached themselves from our gang and prised the boomerang out of Soakum's fingers.

'My dad gave it to me,' Soakum said. Haby was examining the shaft. It was varnished and the grain of the wood ran in a curved pattern around its angle. The boomerang had blue and yellow patterns painted on it.

'Can you make it come back if you throw it? I hear you're gassing too much about its comings and goings.'

'He can't,' some little boys shouted. 'He can only polish it on his pants.'

'I can make it come back,' Haby said.

'You?' Soakum said with unconcealed contempt. 'Only abos and bushrangers can use it properly.'

'If I can, I'll keep it,' Haby said.

He stepped out of the ring of boys and walked authoritatively to clear ground.

'You don't hold it like that,' Soakum said.

Haby was holding the boomerang by its middle. He knew everyone was staring at him. He weighted the instrument like a man putting the shot. Then he held it at knee height.

'If it comes back, I'll keep it,' Haby said.

'It won't come back for you,' Soakum said.

Haby laughed and threw the boomerang vertically in the air. It hung for a moment like a seagull taking the current, and swooped back downward. Haby ran a few steps and caught it.

Everyone except Soakum laughed.

'It's mine now,' Haby said. 'I've proved the law of nature.'

'Give it back,' Soakum said stepping forward to grapple with Farokh.

'Getting nasty, eh?' Haby said and holding the boomerang with both hands now he raised his knee and cracked it in two. He handed the pieces back to Soakum.

'Australians are all daft,' he said.

Then for the first time we heard the cry that was to become famous in school. Soakum began howling. 'Ooooooooooooo,' he sang out. His face turned red and rich tears dropped from his wide eyes.

Extract B

Charity opens help line for school victims of bullying

by Geraldine Hackett

THE CHARITY Kidscape has come across nine cases recently of young girls taking overdoses to escape from bullies, its director, Michele Elliott, said yesterday.

Speaking at the launch by Childline of a telephone help line for victims and bullies, Ms Elliott said that the victims of bullying tend to be intelligent, sensitive and creative.

Most bullying is done by boys and their victims are boys, but Ms Elliott also believes that the scale of bullying among girls has been under-estimated. 'The statistics suggest that bullies divide 80 per cent boys, 20 per cent girls, but I believe it would be accurate to say 40 per cent of bullying is by girls.'

'Bullying by boys is more physical,' she said. 'A 12-year-old was turned upside down in the school lavatory, his glasses broken and his jacket ripped. Girls are more likely to be articulate – they go in for name-calling or *sending a girl to Coventry.

Children who bully are often children who are bullied at home and made to feel insecure, Ms Elliott said. 'They perceive what they see as a sign of weakness in other children and then they attack.'

Ms. Elliott said that she had dealt with a 12-year-old girl who tried to kill herself after being bullied by a gang of girls. The victim had been chased home from school every day; her books had been stolen and her belongings thrown in puddles. 'She didn't show any signs of distress, but her mother came home from work one day to find a note and the girl upstairs in a coma.'

In another case, a 14-year-old girl had been attacked by a gang in the school playground. 'Her mother was so appalled that the school allowed the gang back after being suspended, that she has withdrawn her daughter.'

In a handbook written for the Health Education Authority, Ms Elliott advocates schools setting up pupil 'bully' courts where, under teacher supervision, children can try cases of bullying.

Esther Rantzen, chairman of Childline, cited the case of a 14-year-old boy at a private school who tried to hang himself after he was forced to record accounts of events in his private life and was told the tape would be broadcast at the school dance. His case is among those quoted in a new book on bullying, which was also launched yesterday.

Miss Rantzen told the press launch that 2,000 children had rung for counselling about bullying or being bullied in the two years since Childline was launched. 'Children have a code of honour that they must not tell their teachers, parents or even other children. Childline hopes that the victim of bullying or the bully will perhaps tell a voice at the end of the phone line what they are suffering and be encouraged to find help and protection.

'We have to get across the profound cowardice of the bully, and it is an adult that can make it clear. School swots and sporty types are as likely to be picked on as spotty or fat children,' she added.

Ms Rantzen said that bullies often go on to take part in violent crime or abuse of their wives and children. She urged parents to contact the school head if they suspect a child is being bullied.

From *The Independent*

* 'sending a girl to Coventry' means refusing to speak to her.

Extract C

SOME THINGS TO DO IF YOU ARE BEING BULLIED

- Tell an adult you trust
- Tell yourself that you don't deserve to be bullied
- Get your friends together and say no to the bully
- Stay with groups of people, even if they are not your friends. There is safety in numbers
- Try to ignore the bullying
- Try not to show you are upset, which is difficult
- If possible, avoid being alone in places where bullying happens
- Try being assertive – shout 'No' loudly. Practise in front of a mirror
- Walk quickly and confidently even if you don't feel that way inside. Practise!
- If you are in danger, get away. Do not fight to keep possessions
- Fighting back may make it worse. If you decide to fight back, talk to an adult first
- If you are different in some way, be proud of it! It is good to be an individual

Kidscape, 82 Brook Street,

LONDON W1Y 1YG

1 Using **only** Extract A and Extract B write a **summary** of all you have learned about
(a) bullies
(b) people who are bullied.
Write about 150 words for **each** section.

2 Use ideas from **all three** extracts to complete the following task:
TASK: Continue this telephone conversation between Mary, a Childline counsellor and Terry Soakum.
Mary: Hello, this is 'Childline'.
Terry: Hello, do I have to give my name?
Mary: Not if you don't want to. Do you want to tell me about what's worrying you?
You might like to
- let Terry describe in his own words, the boomerang episode and other things that have happened.
- let him explain how he feels about the school and about bullies.
- let Mary make suggestions how he might deal with the situation.

Write about 250 words.

UCLES 1994

TASK 9

This next example gives you the opportunity to write creatively. The stimulus material below is an article in which Christopher Middleton describes his experiences when he spent a day as a Sandwich Man in Oxford Street in London. It is a very personal piece of writing which is perhaps seeking sympathy.

STIMULUS MATERIAL

It's no picnic being the human filling in a sandwich board on Oxford street. **Christopher Middleton** faces the cruel crowds.

The Sandwich **MAN**

We can never find people to do this,' says the restaurant manageress, strapping me into the contraption. 'They say they can't cope with the rejection.'

What rejection, I wonder, striding out on to Oxford Street? What's so emotionally scarring about walking up and down and handing out a few leaflets?

The answer is not long in coming, as my first attempt to give someone a free-bottle-of-wine voucher is thwarted when she suddenly veers off like an alarmed barracuda. It's not just the desperation with which she avoids me, it's the look on her face. A mixture of pity and horror, as if instead of just a large, red sandwich board, I had a bell round my neck and was shouting, 'Unclean'.

There is something inescapably degrading about being the human filling in a sandwich board. It seems that to allow your own body to be used as a mobile advertising hoarding is only one up from having your hindquarters stamped 'DANISH'. Indian Yogis may seek self-humiliation as a means of achieving godliness, but as the sandwich-board man you are doing it for just five quid an hour.

'Whatever they're paying you, it's not enough,' chortles a man just down from Manchester. 'Dream on,' a group of young men shout, as they catch me peering in the window of an expensive shoe shop. Even England footballer David Platt doesn't want one of my leaflets. 'I'm straight off to Italy after

this,' he says, as his minders hustle him into a sports shop for a book signing, 'sorry.'

The one good thing about being a sandwich-board man is that you are automatically welcomed into the lower strata of Oxford Street society. There is an instinctive common bond with the news vendors, sellers of *The Big Issue*, the handers-out of language school leaflets, even the girls on the ice-cream machines outside the jeans stores. As for the people selling the stolen perfumes and necklaces, they take you, if not into their hearts, at least into their confidence, telling you how many times they've been nicked that day (a £100 fine per arrest).

Then you realise that these people are being nice because they are sorry for you. 'Doing this is bad,' says one hard-faced woman, who's working as a lookout for £3 an hour. 'But it ain't as bad as what you're doing.' Her gum-chewing friends agree, and finger my boards with casual disrespect.

My eyes begin to moisten as, for the first time that day, the boards seem to weigh heavy on my shoulders, the cotton straps cutting into the napkin wedges positioned under my T-shirt. But, just as the rejections from passers-by start to get to me and I am adopting the downward, not-meeting-anyone's-gaze posture that I remember from the sandwich-board men of my childhood, something unusual happens.

A young woman, not pretty, but with kind eyes, comes up to me and asks if she can have one of my leaflets, please.

'Why, yes,' I stammer delightedly. I give her two, three, maybe more – my hands are clumsy with gratitude. She thanks me, smiles, and re-joins her friends. 'Good luck,' she beams.

For the next 30 minutes, my boots are on air, the snubs and refusals no more than gnat bites on my wooden hide. I feel like the Beast with Beauty, or the Hunchback with Esmeralda – 'she gave me water, you know...'

I'm back down with a bump when along comes someone I knew at school. I recognise him straight away; he, not seeing past the sandwich board, doesn't make the connection. However, something obviously clicks because, as he stops to cross the road, he turns round to look at me. Then the 'cross now' bleeping starts up, and he's away with the crowd. I can already hear the mixture of delight and horror in his voice as he tells his wife over dinner that night – 'I'm sure it was him.'

Soon after, it begins to rain.

Handing my boards back to the manageress at the end of the day, I ask her how many leaflets she had given me to take out.

'About 500,' she replies. 'What was your refusal rate?' About ten to one, I tell her.

'Sounds standard,' she says, lifting the boards off my shoulders.

It's only later that I am hit by the full mathematical force of what she has told me. Ten times 500 is 5,000. That's 5,000 fellow human beings saying, 'No.' In one day, that's a lot of rejection.

TASK

Imagine that, for a day, you are doing a job that you absolutely hate. It may be gardening; it may be washing up in a restaurant or café; it may even be babysitting your young brother or sister. Describe your experiences.

Printed over the next three pages are three articles all of which are to do with cars and motoring. They look at current issues and express views. Read them carefully and note what you agree with. Then think through your own ideas on the issues raised. You are going to be asked to write a speech for a debate.

Golden age of motoring loses shine

THE MOTOR CAR was the symbol of affluence and freedom, to which, in the good old days of the open road, almost everybody aspired. but in the growing congestion of the 1990s it has, for many, become a trap. The golden age of motoring is over.

A government drive to control traffic growth has already brought road-building cuts, curbs on out-of-town shopping, restricted access to town centres, hints of similar measures on clogged country lanes and the promise of motorway tolls. Kenneth Clarke, the chancellor, is pledged to raise petrol duty by 5% a year above the inflation rate.

However, a report by the Royal Commission on Environmental Pollution, being published this month, could have even more far-reaching consequences. It wants road-building money to be diverted into public transport; gives warnings of possible charges to enter city centres; and proposes increased duty that could eventually push petrol prices past £5 a gallon.

The impact was calculated for *The Sunday Times* by Dr Steven Lawson, the Automobile Association's head of policy research. The commission's recommendation that duty should be increased 10% above inflation, assumed to average 5%, would bring the price of unleaded petrol from £2.40 a gallon (52.8p a litre) today to £3.57 (78.5p) within three years and £5.03 (£1.11) within six years.

Sir John Houghton, the commission chairman, says it is not against cars and expects such measures will achieve only a reduction in the rate of traffic growth. The report, however, gives a devastating summary of the consequences of uncontrolled growth in vehicle numbers, forecast by the Department of Transport to double in the next 25 years.

The commission envisages huge increases in accidents, pollution and respiratory problems; a sharp fall in the quality of life in towns and villages; the sacrifice of vast swathes of land to new roads; and costs counted in tens of billions of pounds.

The report has already been criticised by motoring organisations but it endorses the concerns of a diverse, growing band of opponents of the annual £2 billion roads programme, including doctors, Treasury officials, Tory MPs objecting to the M25 widening, and the many who feel their lives have been blighted by traffic.

Fiona Reynolds, director of the Council for the Protection of Rural England, said many parents felt the extra cars made it harder to let their children play in streets and walk or cycle to school.

At last week's Tory party conference Dr Brian Mawhinney, the transport secretary, appeared to indicate a further shift to accommodate the commission's findings.

He repeated his predecessor's determination to concentrate road-building on bypasses, to minimise encroachments on open countryside and cities and to drop schemes with serious environmental drawbacks.

In a debate reflecting a swell of Tory shire opposition to new roads after controversial schemes such as the running of a motorway through Twyford Down, Hampshire, Mawhinney went one step further, saying: "Our main priority now should be to manage our existing road network in the most effective manner."

Some observers believe this suggests a possible reduction in the roads programme, at present under review by the Treasury.

Others say it could be linked to the conclusion of another imminent report, from a government committee assessing trunk roads, which shows that building new ones to relieve congestion generates more traffic, so that any benefits are gradually negated.

Dr Phil Goodwin, Oxford University's transport studies director and a member of the committee, suggested last week that road closures should be considered as an alternative way to reduce car use, in view of the success of pedestrianising city centres.

Traffic was growing at a rate that no conceivable road building programme could sustain, said Goodwin. "Supply is not going to keep up with demand and therefore demand has to be brought down to match supply."

One village epitomising the worst effects of traffic growth is Aylesford, Kent, once pretty enough to appear on chocolate boxes but now jammed by drivers using its 13th-century bridge as a short cut between the M20 and the M2. Lorry drivers defy a ban on crossing the bridge and regularly jolt the sides of historic buildings. People in Aylesford say their own cars are sometimes stuck for 15 minutes in the congestion. Windows and walls have to be washed repeatedly and parents blame the fumes for their children's complaints of nausea and dizziness.

Jacky Clayton, whose bay windows have been struck by lorries, said: "The traffic has gone up 500% in seven years and I can't even sit in the garden any more because of the noise." She now intends to move.

Nationally, a doubling of the proportion of children with asthma has coincided with an increase in the number of cars from fewer than 15m in 1970 to more than 25m today. The surge in asthma has prompted intensive studies, which, though providing little evidence that the disease is caused by fumes, confirm that symptoms may be significantly aggravated.

During last week's still, sunny weather, poor air quality was recorded in several cities, with the worst in Manchester on Friday. Dr Malcolm Green, chairman of the British Lung Foundation, said: "It is evident that present air pollution levels are causing bad health and it is important the quality does not deteriorate further. The car needs to be our servant and not our master."

Experts are divided on how to reassert mastery over the motor car. Dr Jeremy Vanke, the Royal Automobile Club's environmental affairs manager, agrees with the commission that car dependence must be reduced by public transport improvements. However, he also supports oil industry claims that although petrol price rises may boost sales of fuel-efficient cars, they will do little to cut congestion.

"Drivers with no choice about how they travel will pay more to do the same. It achieves nothing."

Stephen Joseph, director of the lobby group Transport 2000, said the government was in danger of giving too much stick to motorists, but not enough carrot in the form of alternative travel on buses, trains or bicycle routes.

The effectiveness of the green campaign to turn the government against roadbuilding has alarmed motoring enthusiasts. Paddy Wilmer, a director of the MG Car Club, said: "I don't know whether there really was a golden age of motoring, but we are seeing too many ill-educated attempts at change."

STIMULUS
MATERIAL

To 'D' or not to 'D'

More than 20% of all new cars sold have diesel engines. But should you be considering a diesel? PETER LORIMER investigates.

Noisy, slow, smoky. In the old days it was easy to dismiss diesel cars as all of these things, and 'definitely not for you'. But in recent years, one manufacturer in particular has produced such quiet, quick and smokeless diesels that many motorists have found the benefit of lower fuel consumption impossible to ignore. That manufacturer is Peugeot/Citroën (though the bodies are different, the engines are the same). Lift the bonnet of a diesel Rover Metro, Rover 200 or Rover 400 and you'll also find a Peugeot/Citroën engine.

The attraction of these cars is not merely the fuel consumption. Diesel engines are lower revving than petrol engines, and thus more relaxing to drive. A turbocharged diesel, such as a Citroën ZX Td delivers a hefty slug of power and torque exactly at motorway cruising speeds, greatly enhancing a driver's ability to 'accelerate out of trouble', while the power and torque characteristics of diesel engines are well suited to 'off road' vehicles.

But the main reason diesels have sold in such quantity recently is their high resale value. And, unfortunately, this may now be becoming a little shaky.

High resale values (or 'residuals' as fleet managers refer to them) are as much dependent on perceptions as any real benefit. Diesels are perceived to be more economical to run, so this in itself has enhanced their resale value, which in turn makes long-term ownership a better proposition, which adds to their value.

However, CAP Nationwide Motor Research, publishers of the CAP

Monitor of Future Residual Values, and Lease-contracts, which is a very switched-on leasing company, issued a warning not to overestimate diesel residuals. The more diesel cars in the market, they argue, the less price premium they are likely to command over petrol engined cars.

Furthermore, the true economy benefit of running a diesel car is far less than private motorists realise. With diesel fuel costing much the same as petrol, a private owner driving 12,000 miles a year in a Ford Mondeo Turbodiesel would save only about £175. He would need to have the oil changed more often than with a petrol engine, increasing the 'inconvenience' factor.

Once private motorists catch on to this, they are unlikely to pay the used price premiums of £1,000–£3,000 which diesel cars have commanded over petrol cars. And once that premium is eroded, the total cost of ownership benefits are harder to argue.

So far, most diesel cars on sale at auction have continued to maintain a strong price premium over cars with petrol engines. However, the larger Mercedes diesels have slipped a bit, and with the reintroduction of a 'smoke test' as part of the MOT, buyers have become more wary of high mileage diesel cars.

Diesel or Petrol?

Depending on your type of motoring you may still benefit from buying a new diesel offered at the same price as an equivalent petrol version. If you do a lot of short stop/start journeys, a non turbo diesel can offer a very significant fuel consumption benefit over a petrol engine. This is why most vans and all trucks and buses use diesel engines.

According to The London Bus Preservation Trust, a diesel engined bus does about 10–12 mpg. A petrol engined bus the same size would do about 4 mpg.

If you cover a high mileage and drive slowly (at 40–60 mpg), a non-turbo diesel will also offer a considerable fuel consumption benefit. If, however, you buy the Peugeot 306 Tdi or Citroën ZX Tdi and 'use the performance', your average 'real world' fuel consumption benefit could be as little as 3–5 mpg better than an 1800cc petrol version.

With turbodiesels, much depends on the gearing. On hard-driven journeys I have achieved 49 mpg from a VW Passat TDI estate, 48 mpg from a Vauxhall Cavalier TD; 42 mpg from a Fiat Tipo TD and 41 mpg from a vast Citroën XM TDi estate car, yet only 37 mpg from a Citroën ZX Tdi. The Passat and Gold TDI's are geared at 28.8 mph per 1000 rpm in 5th whereas the Citroën ZX and Peugeot 306 TDi's are geared at 25.3 mph per 1000 rpm. Independent road tests in Diesel Car magazine show the Golf TDI at 52 mpg to have a decisive 12 mpg fuel consumption advantage over the sportier and better-handling Peugeot 306 TDi.

With non-turbo diesels, I would expect to average about 45 mpg in a Citroën ZXD or Peugeot 306D and up to 50 mpg from a Rover Metro diesel. (Over 15,000 miles, I averaged 46 mpg in a Peugeot 205XLD which I bought to benefit from low diesel fuel prices in mainland Europe.) However, owners using small diesel cars in the country reckon on well over 50 mpg from a Peugeot 106D and nearly 60 mpg from a Citroën AXD.

CARS Brian Sewell

MERCEDES-BENZ S350 TURBODIESEL

There was once a time when Mercedes-Benz produced large cars of astonishing, outlandish elegance, with rakish wings, chromed exhausts, frameless windows and Wagnerian presence. These were cars for Valkyries and dragons, cars in which the superhuman heroes of a dark Gothic past might ride roughshod over malevolent dwarfs, cars for gods before the Götterdämmerung. But their descendants have nothing about them to conjure recollections of Siegfried or Brünnhilde, nothing to suggest the Wotan-Wagen with a garage in Valhalla, and are merely large – very large indeed.

With Rolls-Royce slipping from the throne as Best Car in the World (though loyalty, nostalgia and conviction make me feel that the Bentley Turbo version still justifies the claim), Mercedes should be the usurper with its S–class, but it is not, for there is more to being best than brute modernity and a multiplicity of prosthetic aids. Indeed, I might well argue that any old car with a starting-handle has a better claim to the title 'Best' than any with an automatic gearbox. In its most sybaritic guise the big Mercedes has a six-litre V12 engine, against the 6.75 V8 of the Rolls, and in length and width it is a few inches shorter than the Rolls – but mere dimensions take no account of line and bulk, and of these the Rolls has the first and seems the smaller, and the Mercedes the second, and is obese and menacing. Whatever one thinks of the folly of a radiator designed 2,000 years ago as the portico of a Roman temple, it imposes a sense of balanced verticals and horizontals on the rest of the body that gives the Rolls uncluttered elegance, while the Mercedes, with its half-hearted droop snoot and high rump, looks like a compromise between irreconcilable ambitions to be both sports car for Arnold Schwarzenegger and charabanc for the Three Fat Women of Antibes.

Nothing about this Merc's body gives pleasure to the eye: not the wheel arches, which are no shape known to the wheel, not to the fantastical ellipses of speed; not the cutting of the metal to accommodate the lights, which are at haphazard angles unrelated to the form; not even the boot-lid, which has an awkward shape and a tendency to clout the back of the unwary head if not fully opened with resolve – I feel that a small notice, 'You *will* open the boot properly', is in order.

To some drivers, the double-glazing, the doors that shut themselves, the windscreen wipers fit for the Amazon rainforests and other aids (the car is just like a grand hotel where bell-boys assume the guest to be too stupid or too feeble to find the bathroom or operate a light switch) will be some compensation for all this ugliness, but surely even the most technologically-minded of them will deplore the overwhelming drabness of the interior, in spite of fine leather and deep carpets.

I would never thought of reviewing this Merc, which in every way seems a thing of despicably conspicuous consumption and absent taste out of touch with all responsible thinking about the present and future of the car, had I not discovered that it can be bought in Germany (but not here) with a diesel engine. The economy versions available in England are fitted with 2.8- or 3.2-litre six-cylinder petrol engines of languid performance, but the Germans can choose a 3.5-litre turbo-charged diesel that produces far more torque (that is, so to speak, pulling power) than these, reaching its maximum very low down at a mere 2,000 rpm, giving great flexibility.

It may not have the whacking acceleration in the hundreds of the V12, but one stamps on the pedal with astonishing effect at normal speeds, and the huge car sails past lesser metal with aplomb, its automatic gearbox changing down, then up, without a hiccup, the turbo-boost just as subtle as it comes into play.

Only when idling might the passerby tell that the car has a diesel engine, and only at 4,000 rpm might the passenger with a sharp ear detect a note unfamiliar in petrol engines – it is uncannily quiet. This engine is the answer to all accusations of conspicuous consumption in large cars – a diesel large enough to lug a lorry, silenced, smoothed, boosted with a turbo so it can outpace the crowds, geared to give consumption of 30 mpg, and no more polluting than a Mini. Perhaps Rolls-Royce should look at one.

For further details call Mercedes-Benz in Stuttgart on (01049) 711170.

A debate is being held and the motion is, "No family should be allowed to own more than one car." You may choose to be either the principal speaker for the motion or the principal speaker against the motion. Write your speech.

The pages which follow provide advice, in the form of Examiner's tips, on how to tackle the tasks set in this Exam practice section. Read the general points first before turning to the more specific advice given for each particular task.

General Points

On the front of examination papers there is always a certain amount of rubric (advice for you to follow). Always make sure that you read and follow the rubric. Below is a good example:

Pay close attention to what you are asked to write.
PLAN what you are going to write.
Read and check your work before you hand it in.
Any changes to your work should be made clearly.

- Remember that it is a National Curriculum requirement that within any mark scheme there must be separate marks awarded for spelling, handwriting and presentation, so be very attentive to these features of your writing.

- When you are thinking through and preparing your answers do not be afraid to underline and make notes on the examination paper. You may choose to use highlighter pens. What is important is that you think your way through any task before starting to write your answer.

- Make sure that, whatever the task, you include those elements in your writing which distinguish between the pedestrian and the really good – variety of sentence structure including the use of complex sentences, sophisticated vocabulary, perhaps dialogue (correctly punctuated and paragraphed) and so on.

- Look for the number of marks available for a question or task. This is the important sort of clue that you should look for in any examination in any subject. This information will give you a fairly clear idea of the relative difficulty of questions, of the amount of time you should spend on each question and so on.

Task	Examiner's tip
1	• It is very important in writing an answer in the form of an interview that you make sure it does not become a series of one line questions and answers. It is important that the person being interviewed develops points that they want to make.
	• One of the pieces of information on the paper was "Your work will be assessed on the quality of your Reading and Writing". This is a very important piece of information. The examiner will be able to assess your reading skills by noting how well you have understood and used the information in the passage. You will, for instance, have to look carefully at the developing relationship between Frances Ritchie and the young man on the train and, although they only appear at the very end, there might be something to draw out of her relationship with her parents.
2	• The question has not just said "write a summary" but has given you a series of headings which you can use to work your way systematically through the material. Make sure that you deal with each section carefully.
	• Make sure that you use only relevant material and that you do not repeat yourself.
	• Make sure that you use a style of writing which is businesslike and clear.
	• Instructions on the examination paper stated that the purpose of the test was to discover how well candidates could read, write and present information.

Task	Examiner's tip

3

● Use the piece of stimulus material, in this case the opening of *Bleak House*, to give you an idea. What is at the back of this task is the idea that, at the beginning of a novel, it is important to establish the right atmosphere for the narrative. You are asked to link the setting to the place, the weather and the action. To state the obvious, you would probably not start a horror story on a sunny afternoon in your back garden but on a dull, stormy night on a deserted road going past a cemetery.

● With this sort of task do not be afraid to spend anything up to a quarter of your time planning and experimenting before you really get down to writing.

4

You will have noted that each question is worded in a similar way. In the first part you are asked to provide information – "What happens after the writer leaves the cinema?". In the second part you are asked to give an opinion or to give a justification for what you have just said. The second part of each question is certainly as important as the first; you might even argue that it is more important.

5

● Remember that no one sort of writing is any more worthy than another. If you are given a choice, as you are here, it is a genuine choice. So if you know that you are better writing discursively than you are imaginatively, or vice versa, then choose the type of writing which you prefer.

● Candidates were given a lot of choice on this paper – one title out of twenty possibilities. Always make sure that you have read the rubric (the instructions at the beginning of the paper) carefully. Unfortunately candidates have been known to write too many answers on this sort of paper – in this case all three alternatives – or even all twenty choices on the paper (five lines on each!)

6

● This is the sort of task which looks very straightforward but which requires a lot of preparation before writing:

 – read the passage carefully and probably several times,

 – analyse carefully the characters and attitudes of the boy and his mother,

 – think carefully about the purpose of the advice you are asked to give and consider the appropriateness of what you want to suggest,

 – there is no indication on the paper – would you be giving the same amount of advice to the mother and the boy or is there more advice you would want to give the one rather than the other?

● This is from a reading paper which means that the majority of the marks are given for demonstrating a clear understanding of what has to be read. This does not, of course, mean that you should not bother about the quality of your writing or presentation but it does mean that you should refer clearly to what you have read.

7

● Make sure that you have read all the material and have used it.

● The questions expect you to write in different and appropriate styles:

 – question 1 expects you to be brief and to the point,

 – question 2 is asking for a formal letter and so you must set it out properly and write in a suitably businesslike style,

Task	Examiner's tip

> – question 3 is asking you to write for a young people's magazine and so you should use the vocabulary and style which would be right for that sort of publication,
>
> – question 4 is asking you to write a letter but in the form of those letters you find on a "problem page" in an adult magazine so the style would be chattier and helpful.

8

● Again make sure you read all the material carefully. Do not be afraid to spend some time doing this as an examination paper which has been well set will have "built in" the necessary time allowance for that.

● Look carefully at the tasks and the sort of writing which is expected. The first task is asking you to write a summary and it should be in your own words using necessary material from the extracts. The second task is asking you to write a discussion. Who is it between? Make sure that each person sounds different and right.

● For these tasks you are given a suggested word limit. This sometimes happens but not always. Do not waste all your time counting words though. It is quite useful, during your revision, to count the words in something you have written so that you know, before you go into the examination, what 150 words, 250 words and so on looks like in your writing.

9

● What an examiner is looking for here is real engagement with the task. What you must try to convey in your writing is your feelings while doing the job. The aim is to make the reader feel that the experience is real.

● Think carefully of the vocabulary which you use and the sentence structure. You might, for instance, choose to write in fairly short staccato sentences which punch home your thoughts.

10

● You have been asked to write a speech and therefore the style in which you write is very important. You are taking a particular view and it is your job to persuade your audience to vote for you, in other words they must agree with your point of view.

● In a speech, unlike other kinds of writing, it might be an advantage to repeat yourself to hammer home a point.

● You might choose to look straight at your audience and ask them a question or challenge them to agree with you.

● There is quite a lot of material in the articles that you can use but you are always free in this type of task to add views and facts of your own.